EXPERIENCE

HONG KONG

⊙ Walking Eye App

YOUR FREE DESTINATION CONTENT AND EBOOK
AVAILABLE THROUGH THE WALKING EYE APP

Your guide now includes a free eBook and destination content for your
chosen destination, all for the same great price as before.
Simply download the Walking Eye App from the App Store or
Google Play to access your free eBook and destination content.

HOW THE WALKING EYE APP WORKS

Through the Walking Eye App, you can purchase a range of eBooks and destination content.
However, when you buy this book, you can download the corresponding eBook and destination
content for free. Just see below in the grey panels where to find your free content and then scan
the QR code at the bottom of this page.

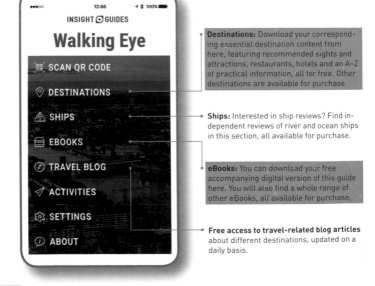

Destinations: Download your corresponding essential destination content from here, featuring recommended sights and attractions, restaurants, hotels and an A–Z of practical information, all for free. Other destinations are available for purchase.

Ships: Interested in ship reviews? Find independent reviews of river and ocean ships in this section, all available for purchase.

eBooks: You can download your free accompanying digital version of this guide here. You will also find a whole range of other eBooks, all available for purchase,

Free access to travel-related blog articles about different destinations, updated on a daily basis.

HOW THE DESTINATION CONTENT WORKS

Each destination includes a short introduction, an A–Z of practical information and recommended points of interest, split into 4 different categories:

- Highlights
- Accommodation
- Eating out
- What to do

You can view the location of every point of interest and save it by adding it to your Favourites. In the 'Around Me' section you can view all the points of interest within 5km.

HOW THE EBOOKS WORK

The eBooks are provided in EPUB file format. Please note that you will need an eBook reader installed on your device to open the file. Many devices come with this as standard, but you may still need to install one manually from Google Play.

The eBook content is identical to the content in the printed guide.

HOW TO DOWNLOAD THE WALKING EYE APP

1. Download the Walking Eye App from the App Store or Google Play.
2. Open the app and select the scanning function from the main menu.
3. Scan the QR code on this page – you will then be asked a security question to verify ownership of the book.
4. Once this has been verified, you will see your eBook and destination content in the purchased ebook and destination sections, where you will be able to download them.

Other destination apps and eBooks are available for purchase separately or are free with the purchase of the Insight Guide book.

CONTENTS

HONG KONG
OVERVIEW

Often compared to Manhattan on account of its urban skyscraper-scape, Hong Kong is at first glance quite like a modern Western city; but it has distinct Chinese characteristics. Take a few turns off its gleaming, dynamic downtown streets, and you'll get an idea of how much tradition is still ingrained.

In the shadows of tower blocks, colourful temples and street shrines bear continually replenished offerings of fresh fruit and burning incense sticks and coils. Teahouses and compact noodle shops are abuzz with as much activity as the more recent additions of coffee-houses and juice-bar chains.

Working Hong Kongers may like their designer togs – and there are malls full of them – but every neighbourhood is home to practitioners of traditional Chinese medicine and vendors of old-school food and snacks, who are kept as busy by young executive types as they are by the older generation.

While Hong Kong is home to the world's second most densely populated island – Ap Lei Chau – and city areas are often thronged with crowds, it takes very little time to find relative tranquillity. Hills appear as if by magic amid the urban sprawl, and trails lead up them towards spectacular views. To discover Hong Kong's lower-rise lush rural pockets, hop on a slick Mass Transit Railway (MTR) train to the New Territories, or take a short ferry ride to one of the more sparsely populated outlying islands.

Back in the city, the famous skyline is best enjoyed at twilight, from the waterfront promenade at the tip of Kowloon, aboard a harbour evening cruise, or from above at The Peak on Hong Kong Island. A nightly light-and-laser display incorporating some of the most prominent, outlandish skyscrapers gives the city a surreal edge.

Street signs are in English and Chinese, English is widely understood in the main neighbourhoods and Hong Kong is one of the world's safest cities – so enjoy.

IN THE MOOD FOR...

.... ARCHITECTURE

Hong Kong is perceived as one continuous skyscraper zone – and this is correct in most urban areas. In 1998, long-standing height restrictions in Kowloon were lifted and since then some very flamboyant structures have gone up – the **ICC Tower** (see page 105) became the territory's tallest building in 2010, soaring almost half a kilometre into the sky. Truly remarkable modern landmarks include Sir Norman Foster's **HSBC Headquarters**, which appears as if its structural rigging is inside out, and the equally spectacular **Bank of China Tower** by I.M. Pei (see page 28).

The few remnants of historic architecture are not so much stunning as evocative of eras past. Both hailing from the early 20th century and worth a look are the stately **Court of Final Appeal Building** (see page 28) and the **Old Wan Chai Post Office** (see page 82). Though built in the last century, the beautifully embellished **Chi Lin Nunnery** (see page 100) is a fine example of much older traditional Chinese architecture, modelled on the classic style of the Tang Dynasty.

.... NO-NONSENSE CANTONESE FARE

Rice is unquestionably the staple of Cantonese cuisine, but dining gets no earthier than a bowl of steaming noodle soup. Noodle shops dot almost every main thoroughfare and small street. Outside Central's interconnecting world of indoor malls, basic noodle shops are sprinkled along Wellington Street and seem never to close along this strip. The best quality bowl is topped with fresh house-roasted duck or goose at **Yung Kee** (see page 60).

For rice with robustly flavoured steamed seafood, braised meat and fresh vegetables, head for the animated dining room at **Lin Heung** in Sheung Wan (see page 60). Dim sum can be another no-nonsense Cantonese dining experience, from breakfast time till early afternoon; it's served at Lin Heung too. Alternatively, try the catch of the day cooked up with ginger, spring onion and soy at the esteemed seafood restaurants lining **Sai Kung** harbour in the New Territories (see page 117).

.... FINE DINING

If Hong Kong does earthy Cantonese food well, its top-tier restaurants are even more critically well received, especially internationally – Michelin food guides launched a local edition in the late noughties.

The jewel in the culinary crown belongs to elegant **Lung King Heen** (see page 35), whose light dim sum sometimes get the surprise addition of a prized Western ingredient. Also top-notch is longer-established **Shang Palace** (see page 92), where you'll enjoy outstanding food and service under its chandeliers. Bridging the gap between Eastern and Western fine cuisine is **Bo Innovation** (see page 39), where the chef's classical French training is applied to deconstructed and re-interpreted Cantonese traditions – with exciting results. No such experimentation at **L'Atelier de Joël Robuchon** (see page 39), where the creations of one of France's culinary kings provide the expected taste-bud wow factor.

Back to the finer side of fusion, with another international celebrity chef: **Nobu** (see page 101). The familiar yet memorable Japanese-meets-South American menu with Western sensibilities is served in an elegant dining room.

.... A NIGHT ON THE TOWN

Once upon a time, visitors to Hong Kong craving a big night out had only the hotel bar or the expat hang-out Lan Kwai Fong to choose between. That's not to say that **Lan Kwai Fong** (see page 40) isn't still a decent night out: the area has a large Chuppie (Chinese yuppie) presence, and it's popular with the partying executive set too.

These days, though, good-timers can take their pick of lively night-spots. Raise the exclusivity factor further just around the corner in **Soho** (see page 56); bars here are often more intimate, and its velvet-roped venues like **Dragon-i** and **Play** (see page 53) are among the hottest nightspots in town.

Raucous, expensive but really buzzing are the banker-crowd bars on the elevated walkway joining Exchange Square and the fourth-floor roof podium at the **Two IFC** tower; a slightly quieter alternative is **Blue Bar** (see page 31). Tsim Sha Tsui is home to happening haunts in and around **Knutsford Terrace** and vibrant Philippe Starck-designed **Felix** (see page 96), which also has a great view.

Speaking of views, loftily perched **Aqua Spirit** (see page 104) offers a panoramic backdrop and theatrical lighting for a Hong Kong cocktail to remember.

.... A QUIET ESCAPE IN THE CITY

As almost no one in Hong Kong has a garden, the city's handful of urban parks are very well used. The clever landscaping of **Hong Kong Park** (see page 32) somehow means it never feels crowded. Relax with a book on one of the benches around the lake, take a break in the café and a stroll through the aviary. Or walk the lush **Wan Chai Green Trail** (see page 82) and within minutes you will find yourself high above Hong Kong Island's bustling streets.

Provided it's not a lunar festival day, larger temples can be sanctuaries: **Wong Tai Sin** and **Chi Lin Nunnery** (see page 100) in Kowloon both have beautifully landscaped gardens and the temple buildings themselves are very easy on the eye. If it's a weekday, catch a taxi or board a bus to the beaches at **Shek O** (see page 141) or **Stanley** (see page 136), which only get busy at weekends and public and school holidays.

.... GETTING SPORTY

Hong Kong is surrounded by the South China Sea, and the weather is warm for most of the year, so water sports are an enjoyable pastime here. Give windsurfing a go on **Cheung Chau Island** (see page 156), or enjoy water-ski and wakeboard sessions on the **Southside** of Hong Kong Island (see page 136). Over in the **New Territories**, hire a surfboard or snorkelling gear and take to the water (see page 120), or rent a bike and explore stunning **Plover Cove Country Park** (see page 123).

.... A LAZY DAY

Soho's laid-back cafés (see page 52) are perfect for whiling away the morning hours. You could then stroll down **Hollywood Road,** popping into antique shops (see page 55) and art galleries (see page 54) that catch your eye. Then board a Hong Kong Island tram and let the driver do all the work; whether you head east or west, sit back and take it all in (see page 41). Follow that with a snaking taxi ride up to **The Peak** (see page 44). Stroll the one-hour flat circular route with its great Hong Kong vistas, or if that's too much effort, grab a drink or meal in a restaurant with views (see page 43).

.... RETAIL THERAPY

No visit to Hong Kong is complete without visiting a mall or three. In fact, city development in the past few decades has made it almost impossible to avoid doing so, as they're often pedestrian thoroughfares.

For those looking to buy top-tier designer brands, **Central** (see page 30) and **Causeway Bay** (see page 84) are home to the glitziest malls on Hong Kong Island, with some top European and US fashion, plus watches and jewellery specifically designed for the Asian market. The **Island Beverley** in Causeway Bay (see page 84) and Tsim Sha Tsui's **Rise Commercial Building** (see page 106) have cutting-edge clothes and accessories from local, Japanese and Korean designers.

Find clothing bargains in over-run shops in Wan Chai's **Johnston Road** (see page 79) and at **Stanley Market** (see page 142), which is also a good souvenir-hunting ground. The best quality Mainland China products, though, come from specialist department stores (see page 102).

.... A PROPER ESCAPE IN A FAR-FLUNG CORNER

You don't have to be a hiker to head up to the **New Territories**. Leave the high-rises behind and aim for **Sai Kung** (see page 121) to see why some Hong Kongers choose to live out in parts that are not dependent on MTR train connections. Mountains, colourful plant nurseries and a village with plenty of cafés, bars and seafront restaurants await. If you want to exercise your leg muscles once you get there, head into nearby inland or coastal country parks for a hike or a snorkel (see page 119). Near-by, **Clearwater Bay**'s fine sand beaches (see page 118), with showers, lifeguards and food kiosks, are very quiet on weekdays.

For a breath of fresh air in what can sometimes be a stifling city, jump on a ferry to one of Hong Kong's outlying islands and watch the city disappear in your wake. In the running for most low-key of all the islands is **Peng Chau** (see page 158). Alternatively, charter a junk or pleasure boat (see page 162) and drop anchor wherever you fancy.

.... BEING ENTERTAINED

Hong Kong Arts Centre and **Hong Kong Academy for Performing Arts** are among the most accessible theatres, putting on the biggest-budget theatre, music and dance performances from local orchestras and production companies (see page 80). Less mainstream performances are held at the independent **Fringe Club** (see page 58) and smaller government theatres across Hong Kong. For a laugh, check out **TakeOut Comedy** or listen to jazz at **Peel Fresco** (see page 58).

.... THE FULL-ON CITY BUZZ

The pace of life in Hong Kong is dynamic. Office workers stride with purpose while talking business on smart phones; shoppers in swanky areas are loaded up with designer bags. Nowhere will you feel this urban heartbeat more than on the main roads of **Causeway Bay** (see page 84), **Tsim Sha Tsui** (see pages 93, 98, 107 and 110) and **Mong Kok** (see pages 97 and 109), where glitzy shops alternate with juice vendors and key-cutters. In **Central** (see pages 28 and 36), it's a mostly upmarket experience – and the buzz is at its peak during lunch hours and early evening.

.... LOCAL CULTURE

A few museums give a great background on Hong Kong's cultural origins: notably, the **Heritage Museum** (see page 122), which spotlights the Southern Chinese ethnic groups that have made Hong Kong home, as well as indigenous beliefs and practices. Get a feel for how much less Westernised Hong Kong once was – from its development as a Treaty Port up to the pre-skyscraper first half of the 20th century – by perusing the photos, illustrations and paintings in the **Museum of History** (see page 95) and **Museum of Art** (scheduled to reopen in mid-2019 after a long renovation; see page 94).

To witness modern-day local culture in action, take a walk around the periphery of **Temple Street Market** (see page 97): fortune tellers give alfresco palm and face readings, restaurant tables are set up outdoors and elderly musicians play folk and operatic music on the pavement.

Take part in two current social passions with a dim sum lunch (see page 35) on a Sunday at elegant **Lung King Heen**, and cheer on your horse on a Wednesday night at **Happy Valley Racecourse** (see page 87).

.... BEING PAMPERED

Spas in Hong Kong's top hotels are ranked among the world's best, and the city is something of a leader in fusing Eastern and Western manipulation techniques and treatment ingredients. Spas at the Hong Kong-based Mandarin Oriental Group have made a point of this with their own house oils and creams – try them at the cosy **Landmark Mandarin Oriental** (see page 46). **Spa at Four Seasons** (see page 46) is possibly Hong Kong's roomiest, with sprawling spaces that house large bubbling vitality pools, steam and shower rooms. **Mira Spa** (see page 34) offers both quality treatments and a refreshingly bright interior and staff demeanour.

Many of these places offer massages and facials targeted at men, but amid all the top-end female-oriented beauty salons in town the ultimate destination for guys who like grooming is the old-school-at-heart Art Deco-inspired **Mandarin Barber** (see page 34).

.... FAMILY FUN

Add an element of excitement to your sightseeing by choosing a fun form of transport. Ride a clunking vintage tram (see page 68); or get hauled up Hong Kong Island's most famous mountain at a weird angle on a funicular railway (see page 41) – with **Madame Tussauds** and the **Chocolate Museum of Hong Kong** (see page 43) waiting at the top; or ride the world's longest series of covered escalators (see page 67). Kids will also love the **Ngong Ping 360** (see page 151), a long cable-car ride above a lush Lantau Island mountain, overlooking islets that dot the South China Sea and aircraft coming and going from the airport.

Hong Kong Disneyland (see page 154) is always a winner with children, and families can enjoy marine life and mammals as well as rides at enduring family favourite **Ocean Park** (see page 145). There's more educational fun at the interactive **Science** and **Space Museums** (see page 95) and the **Railway Museum** (see page 122).

Finally, a trip to Aberdeen's floating **Jumbo Kingdom** restaurant always seems to go down well with the wee set (see page 139).

NEIGHBOURHOODS

Some of Hong Kong Island's swankiest office, shopping and residential areas are found in Central, Admiralty and Mid-Levels, though re-developing pockets of Kowloon are fast catching up. The bars and restaurants of Soho and Noho merge into Hong Kong's premier antique and art gallery area, and westward into earthy Sheung Wan. To the east, Wan Chai and Causeway Bay offer an authentic slice of modern Hong Kong, with some great shopping and nightlife. Just outside all this bustle are the hilly New Territories and outlying islands.

Central, Mid-Levels, Admiralty and The Peak. From the gleaming malls and towers around Exchange Square in Central, which are home to some of the best restaurants in Asia, Hong Kong Island rises through the exclusive residential towers of Mid-Levels up to The Peak. Hong Kong Park and places of worship offer relatively quiet sanctuaries and the Peak Tram whisks you up to the most spacious green enclave of this neighbourhood.

Soho, Noho, Sheung Wan and Western. Soho and Noho, which are abbreviations of South and North of Hollywood Road, sprang up after the world's longest covered series of escalators was built in the early 1990s. Their international cafés, bars, restaurants, small performance venues and boutiques offer cosy and sometimes offbeat diversions. Sheung Wan and Western offer a grittier, more traditional Hong Kong vista of dried foods and herbal medicine merchants, interspersed with newer international-style establishments.

Wan Chai, Causeway Bay and Happy Valley. Restaurants and bars in Wan Chai and Causeway Bay offer some of the territory's best selection of down-to-earth eating and drinking, though there are some highbrow and high-floor exceptions with panoramic harbour backdrops. Causeway Bay pits malls and department stores alongside hipster boutiques. A visit to Happy Valley Racetrack is a great, energising people-watching experience.

Kowloon. Once the earthier side of the harbour, the peninsula of Kowloon still has plenty of no-nonsense neighbourhoods, but its southern tip has some very 21st-century pockets. It's the place to come for markets, museums and magnificent views of Hong Kong Island. A little further northeast are the landscaped grounds of Wong Tai Sin Temple, the most colourful place of worship in Hong Kong, and tranquil Chi Lin Nunnery.

New Territories. The land between Kowloon and mainland China makes up the New Territories – so called as it was ceded to the colonial British government later than Hong Kong Island and Kowloon. Pre-1970s it was mostly arable and livestock farmland; after that, new towns were built to house the growing population. It's still home to villages, country parks, great beaches and spacious temple complexes.

Southside. In contrast to the northern coast of Hong Kong Island, the rocky southern shore remains relatively unspoilt. Stanley has a decent beach on one bay, with restaurants and bars lining another, plus a souvenir and clothing market. The rides and dolphins at Ocean Park remain a major draw and Aberdeen Harbour is immediately recognisable for its flotilla of bobbing junks and sampans housing what remains of Hong Kong's 'boat people'.

Lantau and Outer Islands. A quick ferry ride from the edge of Central lies a low-rise, low-population side to Hong Kong that many visitors don't see. Laid-back waterfront restaurants and a smattering of bars are found on Cheung Chau, Lantau, Lamma and Peng Chau Islands. All offer scenic hikes and good beaches. Lantau's cable car connects with the world's largest outdoor seated bronze Buddha; plus Hong Kong Disneyland is here.

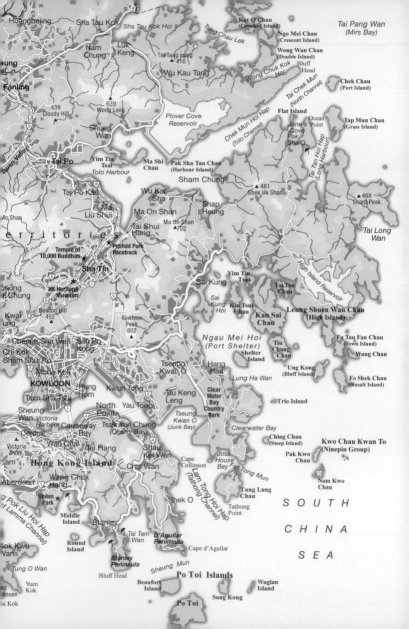

中環
Central

CENTRAL, MID-LEVELS, ADMIRALTY AND THE PEAK

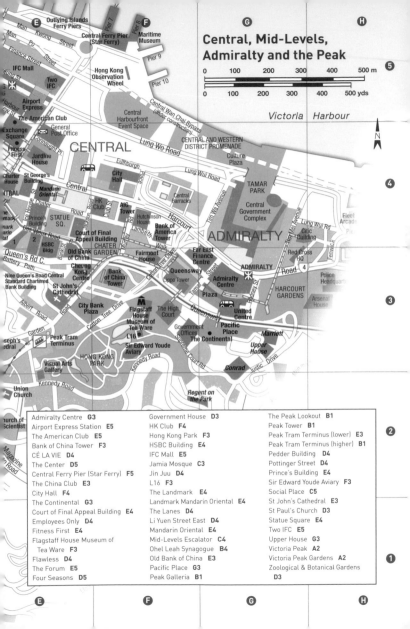

Central, Mid-Levels, Admiralty and the Peak

| 0 | 100 | 200 | 300 | 400 | 500 m |
| 0 | 100 | 200 | 300 | 400 | 500 yds |

Victoria Harbour

Contrast three grand colonial structures with some snazzy skyscrapers

Three of Hong Kong's finest remaining colonial buildings are found in Central district. This traditionally administrative area has also always been Hong Kong's financial hub and premier office address and, as such, it is home to many of the territory's most imposing high-rise towers.

From the 1950s, impressive colonnaded buildings gave way to taller buildings, maximising the same plots of land. That few remain is indicative of Hong Kong's long-standing indifference to heritage preservation.

Thankfully, in the last few years public pressure has forced a closer look at buildings that had been earmarked for possible redevelopment. One of the most precious remaining heritage structures is the government **Court of Final Appeal Building** (8 Jackson Road; map E4) next to Chater Gardens. It opened its stately doors in 1912, when it began life as the Supreme Court Building. Although it became home to Hong Kong's Legislative Council from 1985 until 2011, a statue of Themis, the Greek goddess of divine law and order, has always stood guard outside its main entrance. Assuming you have no official legal business inside, study its arcaded stone exterior with its Greek, European and Chinese features.

Nearby, the **Old Bank of China Building** (2A Des Voeux Road Central; map E3) qualified as a skyscraper when it was built in 1950, but its 17 storeys put it in the shadow of many buildings today. Its style combines late Art Deco and Communist Modernism. Nowadays it houses the China Club (see page 47) and financial offices.

Uphill just above Central is **Government House** (Upper Albert Road; www.ceo.gov.hk/gh; map D3). As the residence of Hong Kong's Chief Executive, it is only open to the public one weekend per year, but its facade can be seen through the gateposts. Twenty-five British colonial governors lived here: Sir John Bowring was the first, from October 1855, and Chris Patten the last.

In contrast to these heritage landmarks is one of Central's iconic modern towers: I.M. Pei's stunning **Bank of China Tower** (1 Garden Road; tel: 2826 6888; www.bochk.com; map F3). At 70 storeys and 369 metres (1210ft) tall, its zigzagging form made it Asia's tallest building when it opened in 1990. At the time it was thought that its sharp angles radiated poor feng shui, but that controversy was short-lived.

A few minutes away is **HSBC Headquarters** (1 Queen's Road; tel: 2822 1111; map E4), a multi-layered glass and metal construction designed by Sir Norman Foster and completed in 1985. At its elevated base are two large bronze lions, originally on guard duty at the bank's former 1935 incarnation.

Rising highest in Central, next to the Hong Kong Stock Exchange, is **Two IFC**, commonly referred to as IFC (International Finance Centre; 8 Finance Street; tel: 2295 3308; www.ifc.com.hk; map E5). Completed in 2003, the building is notable for its 88 storeys – though not designed for public viewing, head to the Hong Kong Monetary Authority Information office on level 55 for a sweeping panorama (Mon–Fri 10am–6pm, Sat 10am–1pm).

A little west from here, office tower **The Center** (99 Queen's Road; map D5) is visible from all directions at night, as its 73 storeys are clad with decorative lighting panels that emit vivid rainbow shades.

Observe *tai-tais* – ladies who lunch and shop – in their natural habitat

Financial crises may come and go, but Hong Kong's high-end *tai-tais* didn't miss a beat. *Tai-tai* literally means wife in Cantonese. But the label is also attached to the top-tier woman of leisure in Hong Kong, who more often than not is married to a wealthy husband or simply born into privilege.

You can observe the fashionable ladies who lunch, and join them for high tea, wherever top designer labels are sold in Central, particularly at the swish shops of **The Landmark** and **Prince's Building**, and at the more exclusive upper-floor boutiques of **IFC Mall.**

Hong Kong's branch of UK department store **Harvey Nichols** in The Landmark is adjacent to Landmark Mandarin Oriental's **MO Bar** (tel: 2132 0077; www.mandarinoriental.com), a *tai-tai* lunch and high-tea hotspot, which since 2018 contains a small enclosed annexe of New York's cult cocktail bar **PDT** (tel: 2132 0110). IFC's **Isola** restaurant (tel: 2383 8765; www.gaiagroup.com.hk) is a handy upscale pit stop two levels below one of Hong Kong's most opulent department stores, **Lane Crawford** (tel: 2118 3388; www.lanecrawford.com). And Prince's Building's sprawling restaurant **Sevva** (25/F; tel: 2537 1388; www.sevva.hk), with its wraparound sofa-strewn wooden-decked terrace, fine pastries and cocktail bar, is owned by one of the glitterati set.

Another favourite *tai-tai* haunt is the **Mandarin Oriental Hong Kong**'s low-lit **Clipper Lounge** (tel: 2825 4007; www.mandarinoriental.com), a long-standing refreshment and chat spot.

The Landmark; 16 Des Voeux Road Central; map E4
Prince's Building; 10 Chater Road; map E4
IFC Mall; 8 Finance Street; map E5
Clipper Lounge; Mandarin Oriental Hong Kong, 5 Connaught Road; map E4

Drink in the deal-making buzz with Hong Kong's movers and shakers

Hong Kong's banking district is home to some lively watering holes. A clutch of bars near Exchange Square is abuzz with an international mix of bankers on weekdays from 5–7pm, once local trading has ended.

Drinkers at **Liberty Exchange Kitchen & Bar** spill through its open front onto the elevated walkway between the Hong Kong Stock Exchange and IFC Mall, creating a similar vibe to banker bars in New York and London.

Glasshouse, atop Two IFC's rooftop podium, is a cracker. Basically a high-ceilinged glass-walled box, it has panoramic views across Victoria Harbour and back, across IFC's elevated garden and into the towers of Central. Grab a tall table at this restaurant-cum-bar, where cocktails are exuberantly shaken every weekday after trading hours. Creative mixes, wine and beer are popular during a discounted happy hour; a bar food menu includes mini pan-Asian rice, noodle and salad dishes. Music is cranked up for early evening; outdoor lounge seating is more chilled, but there's still a dynamic Hong Kong atmosphere.

Nearby, **Blue Bar** at the **Four Seasons** attracts a similar crowd but is cosier than the IFC and

Exchange Square bars. Bag a low-slung armchair or sofa at a window table for a harbour vista. Besides its creative cocktails, several containing small-batch spirits and Asian ingredients, intriguing wines and a decent beer selection are offered. There is an appealing East and West menu, and complementary gourmet snacks are served at tables daily between 5.30 and 7.30pm. The tempo is lifted when a DJ plays live on Friday and Saturday nights.

Liberty Exchange Kitchen & Bar; G/F, Block 2, The Forum, 8 Connaught Road; tel: 2810 8400; www.lex.hk; map E5

Glasshouse; 4/F, Two IFC, 8 Finance Street; tel: 2383 4008; www.gaiagroup. com.hk; map E5

Blue Bar; Four Seasons Hotel Hong Kong; 8 Finance Street; tel: 3196 8830; www.fourseasons.com; map D5

Get an eyeful of greenery at Hong Kong Park

The fenced-in quiet grounds of **Hong Kong Park** are situated a little uphill from most of the Central bustle, and are a calm spot from which to take in the surrounding towering cityscape.

Though it only opened in 1991, the planting of mature trees makes this welcome green space seem as though it's been here for decades. Stretching 8 hectares (20 acres), from above the Lan Kwai Fong party zone in Central to Admiralty, this well-landscaped haven has a water-fall and stream, a central duck pond and benches everywhere – so take a load off your feet and relax.

The fountain near the Admiralty end is crossed by a walkway, allowing for the popular photo opportunity of seemingly walking through it – be aware that you may get a bit wet from the spray. Nearby is restaurant and bar **L16**; its sunken open-sided light wood interior and outdoor garden tables are an excellent quiet spot for a cocktail, meal or cup of tea. If you want to know more about the latter, the **Flagstaff House Museum of Tea Ware** is in the grounds (see page 33), and you can sample a cup of China's finest at its café.

Hong Kong Park; main entrance at 16 Cotton Tree Drive; www.lcsd.gov.hk/parks; daily 6am–11pm; free; map F3
L16; tel: 2522 6333; map F3

Park aviary

The **Sir Edward Youde Aviary** is a highlight of the park. Named after the late Governor of Hong Kong (from 1982 to 1986), its ample netted space gives you the chance to see a rare commodity in Hong Kong – wildlife. Information boards describe the habits of some 100 species of local and regional birds who live in this simulated sub-tropical forest.

Take tea very seriously at the Flagstaff House Museum of Tea Ware

In a quiet nook of Hong Kong Park, towards the Admiralty gate end, the **Flagstaff House Museum of Tea Ware** is a curious find. The structure itself is a rarity – the oldest surviving colonial building in the city, built around 1845, served as the official residence of the Commander of British Forces until 1978. Its whitewashed two storeys with colonnaded porches, against a wall of lush greenery, make it popular with newlyweds as a photo backdrop (there is a marriage registry office within the park).

The permanent collection describes the cultivation of tea, the different brews, how it is processed (immediately dried or fermented first) and the rituals that surround serving it – both in China and beyond.

Frequently changing exhibitions showcase tea-related paraphernalia, from beautifully glazed cups and pots from around the world to drawings and paintings on the subject. Cultivation, serving procedure and a history of teatime implements are all covered. The late collector K.S. Lo donated a collection of prized Yixing teapots in his will in 1995. These fine ceramic pieces are displayed in their own gallery. Alongside exhibitions, the museum holds regular tea gatherings and lectures to promote Chinese ceramic art and tea-drinking culture in tandem.

In the gift shop you get the chance to buy some of the best-quality pots and tea types you might find in Hong Kong. Its café serves premium brews and Cantonese vegetarian dim sum.

Flagstaff House Museum of Tea Ware; 10 Cotton Tree Drive; tel: 2869 0690; www.lcsd.gov.hk; Wed–Mon 10am–6pm, closed public holidays; free; map F3

Freshen up, gentlemen, with a visit to a traditional barber or modern salon

If you're hankering for man-pampering, then you won't have to look far in the Central district – choose between a traditional barber shop or a tranquil spa for a break from the city buzz.

For a timeless wet shave or trim, there is none better than the **Mandarin Barber** shop (Mandarin Oriental Hong Kong, 5 Connaught Road; tel: 2825 4088; www.mandarin oriental.com; map E4). Some of its practitioners have been expertly wielding the soap brush, cut-throat razor, clippers and scissors for decades. In the Art Deco-style waiting area the visitor is offered tea or coffee while sitting in a leather armchair, amid small tasteful displays of the best in global male-grooming products and accessories. Vintage barber chairs and hot towels await.

Gents may prefer to indulge in a facial at **Flawless** (4/F Seabird House, 22–28 Wyndham Street, Central; tel: 2869 5868; www.flawless. hk.com; map D4), a contemporary beauty salon which offers male-specific facials using top British gents' cosmetic brands and massage treatments. Its 'fast male manicures and pedicures' are a nod to the pace of the Hong Kong executive fella.

Over in Kowloon, bright, relaxed and down-to-earth **Mira Spa** at **The Mira** hotel (118 Nathan Road, Tsim Sha Tsui; tel: 2315 5500; www.themirahotel.com; map page 90 C2) offers a men's menu using UK grooming brand The Refinery products. Its Ultimate Face and Body Treatment combines relaxing exfoliation and massage with a refreshing facial.

Be seated for a dim sum experience to remember

A speciality of Cantonese cuisine is dim sum. Small, mostly savoury, dishes – steamed, deep-fried or braised – are eaten for breakfast, brunch or lunch, and usually enjoyed with a pot of tea that is endlessly topped up.

For a modern, approachable take on dim sum, try **Social Place**. Traditional dumplings and small dishes get a twist or two – including both vegetarian (the mushroom bun is a flavourful signature) and sweet options – as they are served from an open kitchen. Booking is essential.

Along the waterfront, elegant **Lung King Heen** at the **Four Seasons Hotel Hong Kong** presents a dim sum menu list that includes refined takes on classics – the *siu mai* combines chopped premium pork, rather than mince, with large crunchy shrimps; there are steamed lobster and scallop dumplings; or baked puffs of whole abalone and diced chicken.

An Admiralty dim sum favourite for decades, **Zen** was shut down in 2013 but re-emerged at a new site in Wan Chai at the end of 2017. The menu consists of light renditions of dim sum classics, such as the rice flour roll with barbecued pork and steamed minced beef ball with bean curd skin. Its old signature of deep-fried chicken wing stuffed with sticky rice and dried shrimp has been deconstructed with a crunchier result.

Social Place; 2/F, L. Place, 139 Queen's Road Central; tel: 3568 9666; http://socialplace. hk; map C5

Lung King Heen; 4/F, Four Seasons Hotel Hong Kong, 8 Finance Street; tel: 3196 8880; map D5

Zen; 2nd floor Garden East, 222 Queen's Road East, Wan Chai; tel: 2868 1883; map page 72 C3

Amble through 'The Lanes' for clothing bargains

The Pedder Building was an anomaly for years: discounted adult fashion, kids' clothing and toys available at a handful of shops in the middle of the CBD – until world-class commercial art galleries moved in from 2013. Two alternative one-stop options for the above, plus sports goods, luggage and homeware can be found in Tung Chung at **Citygate mall** (www.citygateoutlets.com. hk) and at **Horizon Plaza** in Ap Lei Chau (see page 140) – both easily reachable by MTR.

Casual brand-name over-runs can be found along the narrow pedestrian-only streets nicknamed **'The Lanes'** that connect the main thoroughfares in Central district. Formally called Li Yuen Street East and Li Yuen Street West, linking Des Voeux Road and Queen's Road in Central, here you can find bargain clothing (especially for women and children), handbags, accessories and shoes, alongside haberdashery products.

A little further west along Queen's Road, **Pottinger Street** is also worth a rummage. As this cobbled street climbs upward towards Lyndhurst Terrace in Soho, shops line both sides and their vivid wares spill out onto the street, on rails and in boxes. Party costumes are what first catch the eye – this is the place to come to transform yourself into a Chinese empress or Spiderman, or something more scary or festive come Halloween and Christmas time.

The Lanes; Li Yuen Street East and Li Yuen Street West; map D4

Drink in the views with a cocktail at the Café Gray Deluxe bar, or indulge in an overnight stay at The Upper House

Perched on the 49th floor of high-floors-only boutique hotel The Upper House, atop Pacific Place Mall in Admiralty, is a favourite haunt of the well-heeled drinker: **Café Gray Deluxe bar**.

The bar is named after chef Gray Kunz – who was highly regarded in Hong Kong over two decades ago, made it big in the US with Michelin-starred Café Gray, and then returned. The narrow bar joins, but is not fully visible to, Kunz's modern fine-dining restaurant, which has a growing selection of healthy listings. A plate-glass window lined with booths faces the bar counter, and views stretch past the tops of Admiralty's towers, across Victoria harbour to Tsim Sha Tsui. Knowledgeable bar staff serve up lesser-known wine varieties, all simply explained upon request and with plenty available by the glass. There are more familiar choices, too, plus a tempting bar snacks menu.

The hotel itself, a study in the understated by local architect and interior designer André Fu, and with notably on-point service, merits a stay as a treat.

Café Gray Deluxe bar; 49/F, The Upper House, Pacific Place, 88 Queensway; tel: 2918 1838; www.cafegrayhk.com; www.upperhouse.com; map G3

The Continental

Below The Upper House is **The Continental** restaurant (tel: 2704 5211; www.thecontinentalhongkong. com), which compensates for its lack of view with an airy conservatory-like space and terrace garden surrounds, within which seasonal ingredients lead a pan-Western menu. Certain signatures, such as wild kingfish carpaccio with horseradish avocado and mustard oil, and Maine lobster spaghettini, keep diners returning. And the casual bar menu here is a good excuse to try some decent cocktails and wines by the glass.

Grab a top-deck tram or bus seat and take in the sights, sounds and smells of the north shore streets

A trip on a vintage tram as it trundles slowly across the north shore of Hong Kong Island through animated streets, is a great way to feel the pulse of the city – as well as the quickest method of travelling short distances. The tram has changed little since the first generation were launched in 1904. At that time, they were single-decked; the design of the double-decker version used today dates from 1925. Thanks to their windows usually being open,

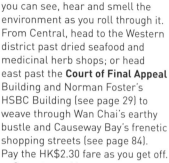

you can see, hear and smell the environment as you roll through it. From Central, head to the Western district past dried seafood and medicinal herb shops; or head east past the **Court of Final Appeal** Building and Norman Foster's HSBC Building (see page 29) to weave through Wan Chai's earthy bustle and Causeway Bay's frenetic shopping streets (see page 84). Pay the HK$2.30 fare as you get off.

Open-topped buses are an easy way to soak up the city with audio commentary. From Central's Star Ferry stop (map F5), **Big Bus Tours'** three routes loop around Central, Soho and along the Wan Chai waterfront, head to the scenic southside or take in the sights of Kowloon; the company runs a short night tour too. Also picked up at a Star Ferry bus stop, **Rickshaw Sightseeing Bus** offers one daytime route with a heritage sites theme and another that focuses on local markets; its night route takes in well-illuminated places of interest. Hop on and off at any point with a day pass.

Hong Kong Tramways; tel: 2548 7102;
www.hktramways.com
Big Bus Tours; tel: 2723 2108;
www.bigbustours.com
Rickshaw Sightseeing Bus; tel: 2873 0818;
www.rickshawbus.com

Become star-struck at one of two Central French Michelin-starred outposts

The Hong Kong dining scene has long been blessed by overseas celebrity chefs opening up outposts in the city. Two Michelin-starred French operations offer a truly world-class experience.

Don't be deceived by the informal air at **L'Atelier de Joël Robuchon**. The service here is slightly sniffy – but that can be excused when food and wine are presented at such an elevated level. Both the tasting and à la carte menus reflect what's in season in France. Expect starters such as caviar-topped crabmeat on a base of tomato jelly and avocado. Its lower-level **Salon de Thé** is a great Continental breakfast spot.

The other top French dining room on Hong Kong Island is **Pierre** at the Mandarin Oriental. Superstar chef Pierre Gagnaire likes to take a key ingredient and serve it in a variety of unusual ways. The langoustine starter, for example, is cooked three ways: served as tartare with sake granite and sautéed mushroom and garlic; poached with diced caramelised pineapple; and grilled, served with citric fruit and endives – and that's all one course. The dark dining room has dramatic views.

L'Atelier de Joël Robuchon; Shop 401, 4/F, The Landmark, 15 Queen's Road; tel: 2166 9000; www.joel-robuchon.com; map E4

Pierre; 25/F, Mandarin Oriental Hong Kong, 5 Connaught Road; tel: 2825 4001; www.mandarinoriental.com; map E4

Bo Innovation

Try the creations of Hong Kong's own Michelin-starred chef Alvin Leung at **Bo Innovation** in Wan Chai (1/F, 60 Johnston Road; tel: 2850 8371; www.boinnovation.com; map page 72 C3). Trained in classic French cuisine, Leung serves up meticulously prepared tasting menus and a boundary-pushing take on Cantonese cuisine.

Party like a young professional in Lan Kwai Fong

Looking at it now, it's hard to imagine that **Lan Kwai Fong,** snaking some 100 metres uphill from Central's Wellington Street, was an unremarkable street until the late 1980s. That's when the first bar with a dance floor opened. Since then, the road gradually became packed on both sides with open-fronted and basement joints, as did adjoining **D'Aguilar Street.**

Though officially different roads, the label Lan Kwai Fong now refers to both. Gradually, buildings of around eight storeys have been pulled down to make way for taller ones that house bars and restaurants. Once an expat haunt, Lan Kwai Fong now attracts mostly local party types and Chuppies (Chinese yuppies).

Nightspots sadly come and go every few years as eye-watering rents here make longevity prohibitive. A betting person might wager on **CÉ LA VI** lasting some time yet,

though. The three-floored restaurant, lounge and rooftop bar at the top of Lan Kwai Fong's most buzzing food and drinks tower gets its groove on with live DJs in the lounge. Creative cocktails often have refreshing elements that befit the lively vibe.

On the ground floor of the same building is atmospheric **Jin Juu,** a contemporary Korean restaurant that also has a branch in London. The lively bar here, offering views out onto the street's revelry, serves imaginative cocktails, often laced with Asian liquor and inventive ingredients.

Employees Only, a New York-style speakeasy bar, was conceived as a Stateside institution for food and drinks industry folk before joining Hong Kong's party hub in 2017. The beautiful interior and expertly made cocktails – classics with minor tweaks – are major draws. The bar-snack list and full menu feature mostly US dishes.

CÉ LA VI; 25/F; California Tower; 32 D'Aguilar Street; tel: 3700 2300; http://hk. celavi.com; map D4
Jin Juu; upper G/F, California Tower, 32 D'Aguilar Street; tel: 2868 9538; http://jinjuu.com.hk; map D4
Employees Only; 19 Lan Kwai Fong; tel: 24682755; www.employeesonlyhk.com; map D4

Get hauled up a mountain through residential high-rises for some unusual perspectives

There is nothing quite like a ride on the **Peak Tram**. Constructed to ease the way up for privileged government officials and executive residents, the tram made its maiden trip in 1888. Formally speaking, it is a funicular railway – steel cable is attached to the cars.

From its terminus between Central and Admiralty, the ascent is immediately steep. At something like a 45-degree angle, passengers are hauled up The Peak on seats facing back towards the direction they've come from. This, and the fact that the tracks cut first through the densely packed residential high-rises of the Mid-Levels district, makes for some unusual perspectives. As Victoria Harbour and Kowloon emerge beyond, the white and pink tiled apartment towers recede to appear as spindly as toothpicks.

Then, near the end of the journey, lush palms, banyans and other vegetation obscure the view – once upon a time, most of the journey would have been like this.

For a different ride back down, consider taking a bus from the terminus at The Peak. This is a slower, winding descent from leafy to urban through a long series of switchbacks, giving a great overview of the city. Check marked bus routes – most of Hong Kong Island is accessed. Or, for convenience, try a cab down.

Peak Tram; St Joseph Building, Garden Road; tel: 2849 7654; www.thepeak.com. hk; daily 7am–midnight; map E3

Feel the faith at one of three houses of worship

Ride up the Mid-Levels Escalator, or walk uphill from Central, to visit the temples of three faiths brought to Hong Kong from abroad. A synagogue, a mosque and a cathedral sprang up many decades ago in this affluent part of Hong Kong, where they serve as hubs of small non-indigenous religious communities. These days, plenty of Hong Kong Chinese join congregations at all three.

In fact, marriages between local couples as well as non-Chinese are common at imposing **St John's**

Cathedral. Well maintained, with whitewashed walls, vivid stained-glass windows, and built in the shape of a cross, Catholic St John's is near the Peak Tram station. Its doors are open daily to the public for quiet prayer or to attend services.

Along the Shelley Street escalator route, through swirling filigree iron gates, is **Jamia Mosque** in a small walled courtyard. Its original mid-19th-century structure, with its small minaret, was the first mosque built in Hong Kong; it was added to in 1915. Islamic visitors are permitted to attend services.

Near here is **Ohel Leah Synagogue**, built in 1902 by a banker, Sir Jacob E. Sassoon, in memory of his mother, Leah. The Eastern Jewish-style building has two storeys to enable female worshippers to be seated in a balcony area. Its renovation in 1998 won a heritage award from Unesco. Services are held daily.

St John's Cathedral; 4–8 Garden Road; tel: 2523 4157; www.stjohnscathedral. org.hk; Mon–Tue & Fri 7am–6pm, Wed 7am–6.30pm, Thu 7am–5pm, Sat–Sun 7am–7.30pm; map E3
Jamia Mosque; 30 Shelley Street; tel: 2523 7743; daily 9am–8pm; map C3
Ohel Leah Synagogue; 70 Robinson Road; tel: 2589 2621; www.ohelleah.org; Mon–Sat 7am–7.30pm, Sun 8am–7.30pm; map B4

Eat on The Peak's historic terrace

Head up to **The Peak Lookout** to start your day with a breakfast or lunch that is very fairly priced for its quality and location. Take your seat on the terrace or in the conservatory, and revel in the glorious views.

The restaurant's main building is a heritage site that dates back to the last years of the 19th-century, when it went up as an open-sided shelter for public and private sedan chairs – then the only means of getting up and down the hillside. In 1947 it was converted into a café. History aside, the menu is a mix of Asian and Western dishes; its tandoor-oven items are standouts, and its tiered, chilled seafood platter has been a signature for years.

Half a day can be pleasantly whiled away up here. Kids – and adults – will be entertained by lookalikes at the small waxworks museum **Madame Tussauds**: strike a pose with Bruce Lee, Johnny Depp, Lady Gaga and a host of other international and local entertainment celebs, sports stars and supermodels. Alternatively, check out the **Chocolate Museum of Hong Kong**, a niche display of outlandish paintings, large wall-hung reliefs and sculptures of Chinese dragons, dinosaurs and seasonally changing items all made of... white, milk and dark chocolate; check the website for sporadic hands-on choc-art workshops. Then take a bus or minibus back down for a white-knuckle ride along snaking, hill-hugging roads.

The Peak Lookout; tel: 2849 1000; www.peaklookout.com.hk; map B1
Chocolate Museum of Hong Kong; 208-2092/F, Peak Galleria, 118 Peak Road; tel: 2882 0488; www.theartofchocolate.com. hk; Mon–Thu 10am–9pm, Fri–Sun until 10pm; map B1
Madame Tussauds; Shop P101, The Peak Tower, 128 Peak Road; tel: 2849 6966; www.madametussauds.com/hong-kong/en; daily 10am–10pm; map B1

Take aim for World War II remains and lush walking trails on The Peak

There are a variety of superb walks from the Peak Tower. **The Peak Trail** follows Lugard and Harlech roads to complete a circuit of Victoria Peak, affording magnificent views across the harbour and Kowloon to the north, Cheung Chau and Lantau to the west, and the great masses of junks and sampans at Aberdeen to the south, with Lamma Island beyond. This gentle 3km (1.8-mile) walk, well signposted and shaded from the sun, takes about 50–60 minutes round trip from the Peak Tower.

The area around the Peak Tower is in fact **Victoria Gap,** whereas the summit of Victoria Peak itself (552 metres/1810ft) lies to the west. Follow the Peak Trail until you reach Mount Austin Road, which winds up to the attractive **Victoria Peak Gardens.** The summit itself, with its pair of radio towers, is out of bounds. The whole area is rich with botanical and ornithological interest. Two of the most common sightings are the Pacific swift and Asian house martin, while kites and eagles often glide above, searching for their next meal.

You might also visit the largely intact remains of **Pinewood Battery**, which lie off the more visited paths on Victoria Peak. At 307 metres (1007ft), it was the city's highest coastal defence artillery platform. In the 1920s, anti-aircraft defence guns were fitted, and subsequently used during World War II. Some underground tunnels and barracks foundations remain, and information boards describe some of the missing structures.

It is possible to walk back down to Central and enjoy some of the finer views and footpaths through The Peak's wooded slopes. The **Central Green Trail** – marked by 14 bilingual signboards highlighting points of interest – winds its way down from Barker Road, across May Road and then via paths named Clovelly, Brewin and Tramway back to the Garden Road terminus. Be prepared for the occasional steep ascent and allow around three hours for a comfortable walk up. Along the way you might see frogs, small snakes or even a wild boar.

Another short, steep route through the forest, signposted to the Mid-Levels, descends northwards from Findlay Road (just below the Peak Tower) to the beginning of the Old Peak Road. A popular longer walk descends westwards through Pokfulam Country Park, and constitutes Stage 1 of the **Hong Kong Trail**. For more ambitious hikers, the rest of the trail heads east for some 50km (30 miles) all the way to Tai Tam and on to Shek O. Nature-lovers can wander through forests of bamboo and fern, stunted Chinese pines, hibiscus and vines of wonderful, writhing beauty. Ornithologists log sightings of birds such as blue magpies and crested goshawks.

The Peak; map A1–B1

Invest in quality wellness time at one of the city's best gyms and spas

If keeping fit or being pampered is part of your holiday routine, you're in luck. Hong Kong's top-end gym and spa scene is up there with the best of them.

Pure Fitness has four gyms worth dropping into in Central, though its IFC one (Mall Level 3, Two IFC, 8 Finance Street; tel: 8129 8000; www.pure-fit.com; map E5) is more spacious; contemporary equipment, knowledgeable attendants and a clean environment make it a winner. They offer various short-term packages, too. **Fitness First** (37/F, One Exchange Square; tel: 3106 3000; www.fitnessfirst.com.hk; map E4), with other branches around Hong Kong, is another top-end gym with day passes available.

Top spas are, unsurprisingly, found in some of the most highly rated hotels. The **Oriental Spa** (The Landmark Mandarin Oriental; 15 Queen's Road; tel: 2132 0011; www.mandarinoriental.com; map E4) is the antithesis of its mid-Central location. Book a drop-in class at the serene yoga and pilates studio; or head to the tranquil spa, heat rooms and whirlpools. Spa treatments combine Eastern and Western techniques, using premium essential oils.

The Oriental's Digital Detox Retreat is the perfect antidote to the fast pace of modern life. Visitors are required to check in their smartphone to escape distractions and enjoy the moment, starting with an unwinding and detoxifying foot ritual, followed by a deep massage. House oils blended by the UK's Aromatherapy Associates and the focus of the massage are determined in a pre-treatment consultation.

Spa at Four Seasons (6/F, 8 Finance Street; tel: 3196 8900, www.fourseasons.com; map D5) is unusually spacious and airy for Hong Kong. Do arrive an hour before a treatment to get into the calm zone – try out its sauna and steam rooms, 'experience' showers, vitality pool and relaxation area. The Vital Energy Crystal Healing treatment claims to achieve otherworldly levels of relaxation using a house Ayurvedic oil blend, hands-on healing, sound therapy (via singing bowls) and selected crystals.

Hobnob with the club set at one of a handful of members-only establishments

A few clubs in Central allow you to mingle with Hong Kong's movers and shakers – and even though they're members-only, a good concierge can help get you in.

One of the oldest establishments is **The Hong Kong Club**, which launched in 1846 as the first colonial club in Hong Kong. Now housed in a curvaceous tower, though still on its original site overlooking Victoria Harbour and back to The Peak, members enjoy restaurants, a gym, squash courts, a billiards room and bowling alleys.

In the Old Bank of China Building (see page 28), **The China Club** is a real pleasure to visit. Its interior is a study in Shanghai Art Deco, and the walls and sculpture plinths display the art collection of its founder-owner, Sir David Tang. The Long March Bar has a wooden decked terrace with a spectacular skyscraper and harbour view.

The American Club of Hong Kong has a country-club annexe too, but the main branch, spaciously spread over two high floors above the Hong Kong Stock Exchange, does hospitality just right. Cityscape and harbour views are jaw-dropping from its handful of restaurants and bars.

The Hong Kong Club; 1 Jackson Road; tel: 2525 8251; map F4

The China Club; 13/F, Old Bank of China Building, Bank Street; tel: 2521 8888; map E3

The American Club; Two Exchange Square; tel: 2842 7400; www.americanclubhk.com; map E5

SOHO, NOHO, SHEUNG WAN AND WESTERN

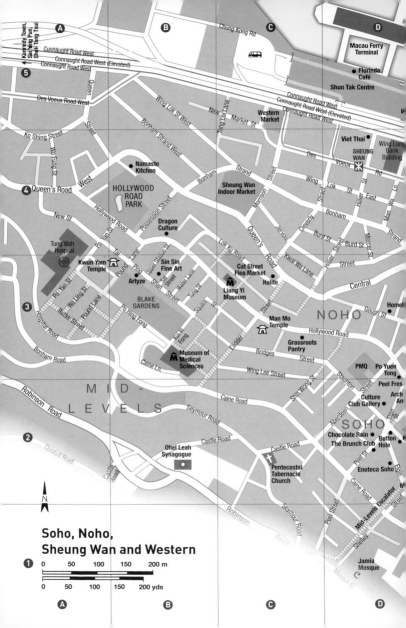

Soho, Noho, Sheung Wan and Western

Chung Kong Rd

Connaught Road West
Connaught Road West (Elevated)
Connaught Road West

Kennedy Town,
Sai Ying Pun,
Shek Tong Tsui

Des Voeux Road West

Macau Ferry Terminal

Florinda Café

Shun Tak Centre

Connaught Road West
Connaught Road West (Elevated)
Connaught Road West

Ko Shing Street

Wing Lok St West

New Market St

Tung Lok Lane

Western Market

Des Voeux Road West

Queen Street

Bonham Strand West

Wo Fung Street

Bonham Strand

Namaste Kitchen

HOLLYWOOD ROAD PARK

Possession Street

Sheung Wan Indoor Market

Bonham Strand

Morrison Street

Des Voeux Road

Wing Lok Street

SHEUNG WAN

Viet Thai

Wing Lung Bank Building

Queen's Road

New Street

Hollywood Road

Ladder Street

Tai Ping Shan Street

Upper Station Street

Dragon Culture

Lok Ku Road

Bonham Strand

Cleverly Street

Jervois Street

Burd St

Burd St

Hillier Street

Morrison Street

Mercer Street

Central

Tung Wah Hospital

Po Yan Street

Kwun Yam Temple

Sin Sin Fine Art

Artyze

Cat Street Flea Market

Liang Yi Museum

Halite

Queen's Road

Kwai Wa Lane

Gough St

Homel

Hospital Road

Wa Ling St

Pound Lane

Rutter Street

BLAKE GARDENS

Po Hing Fong

Ladder Street

Square Street

Shin Hing Street

Man Mo Temple

NOHO

Bonham Road

Caine Lane

Museum of Medical Sciences

U Lam Terrace

Wing Lee Street

Bridges Street

Hollywood Road

Grassroots Pantry

Staunton Street

PMQ

Po Yuen Tong

Peel Fres

Robinson Road

MID-LEVELS

Seymour Road

Caine Road

Shing Wong St

Aberdeen Street

Culture Club Gallery

Arch An

SOHO

Conduit Road

Ohel Leah Synagogue

Castle Road

Castle Road

Pentecostal Tabernacle Church

Elgin Street

Chocolate Rain

The Brunch Club

Button Hole

Enoteca Soho

Robinson Road

Seymour Road

Peel Street

Caine Road

Mid-Levels Escalator

Shelley Street

N

**Soho, Noho,
Sheung Wan and Western**

0   50   100   150   200 m
0   50   100   150   200 yds

Jamia Mosque

Mosque St

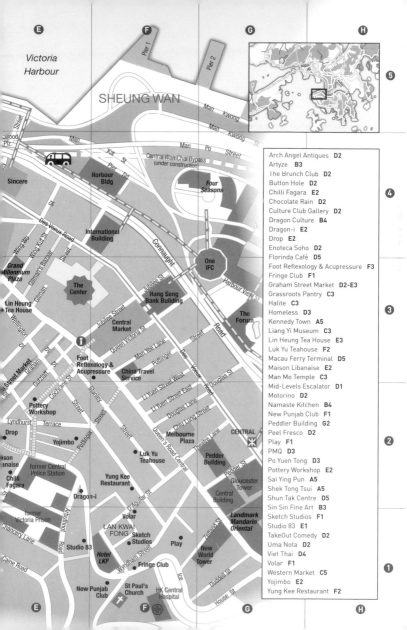

E · F · G · H

Victoria Harbour

SHEUNG WAN

5

4

3

2

1

Pier 1

Pier 2

Man Kwong

Man Kwong St

Man Po Street

Man Street

Kat St

Pier Rd

Central Wan Chai Bypass (under construction)

Connaught

Harbour View St

Rumsey Street

Des Voeux Road

Connaught Road

Wing Lok St

Wing Kut St

Cleverly St

Gilman's Bazaar

Jubilee Street

Hang Seng Bank Building

One IFC

Four Seasons

The Forum

Sincere

Harbour Bldg

International Building

The Center

Grand Millennium Plaza

Lin Heung Tea House

Wellington St

Gilman St

Graham St

Cochrane Street

Gutzlaff St

Jubilee Street

Central Market

Queen Victoria St

Man Yee Lane

Pottinger St

Li Yuen Street West

Li Yuen Street East

Li Yuen Lane

Douglas St

Douglas Lane

Chiu Lung Street

Des Voeux Road

Stanley St

China Travel Service

Foot Reflexology & Acupressure

Queen's Road Central

Theatre Lane

Melbourne Plaza

Pedder St

Pedder Building

Gloucester Tower

Central Building

CENTRAL

Po Street Market

Pottery Workshop

Drop

Yojimbo

Lyndhurst Terrace

Maison Libanaise

Chilli Fagara

Dragon-i

former Central Police Station

former Victoria Prison

Chancery Lane

Caine Road

Studio 83

Hollywood Road

Aberdeen Street

Peel Street

Elgin Street

Staunton Street

Yung Kee Restaurant

Volar

LAN KWAI FONG

Sketch Studios

Hotel LKF

Play

Fringe Club

New World Tower

Landmark Mandarin Oriental

Wyndham Street

D'Aguilar St

Wellington St

New Punjab Club

St Paul's Church

HK Central Hospital

Ice House St

Duddell St

Wyndham St

Arch Angel Antiques	D2
Artyze	B3
The Brunch Club	D2
Button Hole	D2
Chilli Fagara	E2
Chocolate Rain	D2
Culture Club Gallery	D2
Dragon Culture	B4
Dragon-i	E2
Drop	E2
Enoteca Soho	D2
Florinda Café	D5
Foot Reflexology & Acupressure	F3
Fringe Club	F1
Graham Street Market	D2-E3
Grassroots Pantry	C3
Halite	C3
Homeless	D3
Kennedy Town	A5
Liang Yi Museum	C3
Lin Heung Tea House	E3
Luk Yu Teahouse	F2
Macau Ferry Terminal	D5
Maison Libanaise	E2
Man Mo Temple	C3
Mid-Levels Escalator	D1
Motorino	D2
Namaste Kitchen	B4
New Punjab Club	F1
Peddler Building	G2
Peel Fresco	D2
Play	F1
PMQ	D3
Po Yuen Tong	D3
Pottery Workshop	E2
Sai Ying Pun	A5
Shek Tong Tsui	A5
Shun Tak Centre	D5
Sin Sin Fine Art	B3
Sketch Studios	F1
Studio 83	E1
TakeOut Comedy	D2
Uma Nota	D2
Viet Thai	D4
Volar	F1
Western Market	C5
Yojimbo	E2
Yung Kee Restaurant	F2

Laze over a delectable weekend brunch in Soho

A leisurely brunch at a Soho café or restaurant is a great way to kickstart a relaxing Saturday or Sunday.

As its name suggests, **The Brunch Club** (70 Peel Street; tel: 2526 8861; www.brunch-club.org; map D2) makes brunch its *raison d'être*, and serves up an à la carte menu daily, and then separate lunch and dinner menus after that. Its delicious omelettes, crêpes, quality coffee and fresh juices make it very popular at weekends.

Maison Libanaise (10 Shelley Street; tel: 2111 2284; www.maison libanaise.com.hk; map E2) serves good, Middle Eastern dishes that are enjoyable throughout the week, but suit the weekend brunch slots very well, as its gently buzzing tables attest. Pan-fried halloumi, roast cauliflower with harissa or lamb kofta anyone? A changing selection of Lebanese wines graces the drinks list.

A restaurant with a pretty unusual weekend brunch spread is **Uma Nota** (38 Peel Street; tel: 2889 7576; www.uma-nota.com; map D2). Their Brunch da Rua, like the restaurant's à la carte menu, reflects its Brazilian and Japanese hybrid cuisine. *Polvo ao vinagrete* or vegetarian ceviche is served as a fresh start, followed by individual *pastéis* (Brazilian-style fried won ton) or *dadinhos de tapioca*. Round off the main course (think slow-cooked pork ribs, seabass in banana leaf and grilled flank steak) with a shared dessert. Take your time in the warm light-filled surrounds – and consider a table with a sofa.

A tasty wholesome breakfast is served every day at vegetarian **Grassroots Pantry** (108 Hollywood Road; tel: 28733 353; www.grass rootspantry.com; map C3), and its long weekend brunch is accompanied by a very chilled vibe. The menu features unprocessed local, sustainable and organic ingredients within Western and Asian dishes. Select from the likes of scrambled tofu or eggs with sautéed mushroom and spinach, courgette and carrot slaw; Koji smoked carrot crepes with shaved Chinese seasonal greens and pine-nut mousse; and acai berry cacao bowl with coconut yoghurt, mixed toasted seeds and dry and fresh fruits. The coffee selection suits all preferences.

Hit Soho's exclusive nightclubs where top DJs take to the decks

Plush decor with opulent lighting and a pumping sound system; beautifully coiffed young men and women laughing into their champagne flutes; other revellers cutting loose on a small dance floor. This scene is replayed over and over again in Soho's de rigueur nightspots.

Play (1/F, On Hing Building, 1 On Hing Terrace; www.playclub.asia; map F1), on the border of Soho and Lan Kwai Fong party zone, is one of the few places where large format bottles of champagne can be ordered. Should the cocktail of dancing and drinking not be enough, keep a look out for a live guest drop in – Kelis, Sean Kingston and Grandmaster Flash have all taken a turn here.

Velvet ropes can be tough to pass at **Dragon-i** (The Centrium, 60 Wyndham Street; tel: 3110 1222; www.dragon-i.com.hk; map E2) on weekend nights; it's long been a party spot for Hong Kong's models and uber-moneyed 30-plus crowd.

Regular overseas big-name DJs and occasional live musicians perform.

Dance music types should head for **Volar** (Basement, 38–44 D'Aguilar Street; tel: 2810 1510; www.volar.com.hk; map F1), though, again, it can get tough on the door. The best of local and overseas DJ talent spins and, as of 2018, a sound-activated LED system completes the picture.

Tiny **Drop** (Basement, On Lok Mansion, 39–43 Hollywood Road; tel: 2543 8856; map E2), a very cool mini-club co-founded by a great Hong Kong DJ, Joel Lai, is easier to get into earlier in the evening. Later, its members get priority.

The newer kid on the block, **Yojimbo** (upper G/F, Car Po Commercial Building, 43 Pottinger Street; tel: 2576 1717; www.yojimbo.com.hk; map E2) opened at the end of 2017 and proved an instant hit. The club has a Japan-inspired cyber-age interior, with a number of fun Japanese cocktails listed.

Take in edgy visual arts by local and global emerging talents in a clutch of intimate galleries

A vibrant arts scene exists in Hong Kong, and you will find pockets of creativity throughout the territory.

On the edge of gallery-studded Hollywood Road and Wyndham Street is the **Fringe Club**, which has three small galleries. These are sometimes hired out to show non-Hong Kong artists, but more often they show home-grown work by an international mix of creative residents, many of whom are not full-time artists.

Sin Sin Fine Art, founded by local fashion and jewellery designer Sin Sin Man, champions contemporary Indonesian painters, sculptors and printmakers, with a few upcoming mainland Chinese and Hong Kong artists – and occasional international ones – also appearing. Musical performances are periodically staged here, and there is a second gallery in Wong Chuk Hang (Aberdeen).

For edgy European, Asian and Middle Eastern street art and graffiti, as well as several pieces employing plenty of tongue in cheek, **Artyze** is the place to go. It's located just downhill from Hollywood Road into Poho – an annoying recent neighbourhood tag for the creatively developing area around the quietish street of Po Hing Fong.

If you're planning to visit in March, and appreciate fine art, check what's on at Hong Kong's annual **Art Central** (http://artcentral hongkong.com). It used to focus on up-and-coming practitioners, with plenty from Asia, but as of 2018 became more interested in established international artists – possibly a result of competition from **Art Basel Hong Kong** (www.artbasel. com/hong-kong), which also takes place in March. Art Basel is worth seeking out for an overview of some of the world's most sought-after modern and contemporary works.

Fringe Club; 2 Lower Albert Road; tel: 2521 7251; www.hkfringe.com.hk; Mon–Sat noon–midnight or later; map F1

Sin Sin Fine Art; 52 Sai Street, Sheung Wan; tel: 2858 5072; www.sinsin.com.hk; Mon–Sat 9.30am–6.30pm; map B3

Artyze; 32–34 Tai Ping Shan Street; tel: 9761 3103; www.artyze.com; Fri 6pm–9pm, Sat 1pm–6pm; map B3

Discover an Asian antique or vintage artefact around Hollywood Road

There are a slew of antique dealers on Hollywood Road and Wyndham Street, and in the main they offer genuine, ethically procured objects from China and Asia. Good dealers are fonts of information and should be happy to provide a certificate of authenticity from the Hong Kong Art Craft Merchants Association if you're buying an expensive piece.

Most are on Hollywood Road, which stretches from Central to Sheung Wan districts. In business for more than two decades and considered reputable is antiques shop **Po Yuen Tong** (no. 70), specialising in ceramics and bronzeware. **Arch Angel Antiques** (no. 53–5) has a large and varied selection. Many pieces at **Dragon Culture** (no. 231), such as its Han Dynasty terracotta and sculptures from other eras, are considered to be museum-quality. The gallery is now in its fourth decade and owner Victor Choi is a published authority on Chinese antiques.

For a rotating selection of Chinese Ming and Qing Dynasty fine antique furniture and European and Asian silverware and bejewelled accessories, be sure to pay a visit to the appointment-only **Liang Yi Museum** (no. 181–199; tel: 2806

8280; www.liangyimuseum.com; Tue–Sat 10am–6pm; map C3).

Along Hollywood Road, a few shops and street stalls sell vintage Communist-era paraphernalia, like Mao Zedong badges, cups, copies of the *Little Red Book* and toys made of tin. In the Cat Street and Ladder Street area, just downhill from Man Mo Temple, you'll find old reproduction photos of Hong Kong and mainland China, as well as real and reproduction 'smoking posters' – collectable early- and mid-20th-century advertising prints.

Hollywood Road; map A4–D2

Feast on world food while people-watching in the atmospheric restaurant and bar zone

Since the Mid-Levels escalator was built in the early 1990s, all manner of shops, bars, cafés and restaurants mushroomed around it in Soho and Noho, capitalising on the captive market of standing pedestrians. Over the years, the neighbourhood has built up a reputation as an international restaurant and bar zone.

Soho's main eating and drinking thoroughfares are the first two streets parallel to and uphill from Hollywood Road: Staunton Street and Elgin Street. Both sides of these are lined with establishments, broken up occasionally by fashion or ceramic and homeware stores. In recent times, Wyndham Street has become the new kid on the block, with its art galleries and antique shops making way for see-and-be-seen-in bars and restaurants.

For a prime people-watching spot – the escalator travels right past the open French windows – and one of the best renditions of authentic New York-style Neapolitan pizza, pop into **Motorino** (14 Shelley Street; tel: 2801 1668; www.motorinopizza.com; map D2), whose first outlet opened in Brooklyn. Its Brussels sprouts, smoked pancetta and garlic is a legendary recipe, and the meatball, cheese and tomato is also inspired. There is a weekday set lunch here

that's reasonably priced and service is friendly.

Away from the throng, an elegant throwback to post-colonial India and Pakistan opened in 2017: the **New Punjab Club** (34 Wyndham Street; tel: 2368 1223; http://new punjabclub.com; map F1). Moustachioed waiters, dressed in early 20th-century-style braided jackets, bring drinks trolleys to the table for G&Ts or scotch to get things started. Menu-wise, elevated versions of traditional dishes found in the Punjab regions of India and Pakistan are served, with some modern flourishes. Smashed samosas with tamarind sauce and mint raita, and

scattered with pomegranate, looks artful; the signature tandoori lamb (prime New Zealand cuts) comes with beetroot korma and roast onion – a winning combination.

You won't go short of Chinese food round here either. **Chilli Fagara** (7 Old Bailey Street; tel: 2796 6866; www.chillifagara.com; map E2) has been offering Sichuan provincial dishes, with their mouth-numbing pepper-enhanced seasoning, to great acclaim since 2005 – moving to a larger Soho location in 2015 to accommodate its success. Try the award-winning Pearl of the Orient: a grain-fed chicken breast is used to wrap and preserve the sweetness and juice of a long-an fruit, which is similar to a lychee. Noodle and soup dishes here are superior. Grab a beer served traditionally, in a ceramic bowl rather than a glass; wine is also served.

Enoteca Soho (47 Elgin Street; tel: 2525 9944; map D2), an Italian small plates specialist with a very respected European wine list, is another established favourite. With several by-the-glass options and the likes of herbed fish goujons with chilli-lemon aioli, smoked paprika pork skewers with sherry-vinegar sauce, it's easy to while away an evening gazing through its open front onto one of Soho's main dining streets.

Be entertained with music, comedy and other live performances at a small Soho venue

A few years ago, a night of live entertainment in Hong Kong meant waiting for one of the annual arts festivals to come around, sporadic visits to a large auditorium for mainstream productions or taking in a smaller show at the **Fringe Club** (see page 54; 2 Lower Albert Road; tel: 2521 7251; www.hkfringeclub.com; Mon–Sat noon–midnight or later; map F1). Housed in the various buildings of an old colonial dairy, the Fringe remains one of Hong Kong's foremost centres for alternative arts, with a small theatre and studio, and a bar stage that hosts

musicians on weekend nights, but it has been joined by other small-scale venues and arts spaces in the neighbourhood.

Peel Fresco Music Lounge (49 Peel Street; tel: 2540 2046; peel-fresco.com; map D2) has carved out a niche for itself as a jazz and blues bar – and it attracts the best of a core of respected Hong Kong jazz musicians. International performers drop in for gigs from time to time.

Culture Club Gallery (15 Elgin Street; tel: 2127 7936; www.culture club.com.hk; map D2) has morphed from being an art gallery into a cosy gig venue. Check its website as the roster is sporadic; it also holds tango classes (drop-ins welcome) and serves food and drink. And somehow, it still changes the fine art hanging on its walls – mostly by local artists – every few months.

Local stand-up comedians have been making their mark since the late 1990s at **TakeOut Comedy** (Basement, 34 Elgin Street; tel: 6220 4436; www.takeoutcomedy. com; map D2). Most nights have English-language comic and improvisation acts, with occasional appearances by Cantonese performers.

Get creative in Soho and Noho – the increasingly bohemian parts of town

Hollywood Road, Soho and Noho are strewn with art galleries, antique shops and a smattering of edgy boutiques. Within this hub of creativity, it's possible to roll up your sleeves and leave your own artistic stamp at a neighbourhood art studio.

While others have sadly fallen by the wayside in this high-rent neighbourhood, **Studio 83** has become the go-to creative space. Begun as a smaller group-painting venue, it now also offers group and individual workshops, tailored to leaving you on your own or with a teacher to sketch, paint in oil, acrylic or watercolour on a scale and timeframe of your selection.

For something a little more zany, painting under 'black-light' or UV-lighting is offered at **Sketch Studios**, a few minutes' stroll from Soho in Lan Kwai Fong party-zone. Canvases are just one option for would-be brightly coloured artwork: choose from masks, headbands, bracelets and sunglasses. Given its vibe and location, sessions can feel more like a party than being in an art studio – and BYO drinks are welcome with no corkage charge.

If 3D art is more your thing, get behind a wheel at **The Pottery Workshop**. You can book one ses-sion or more with studio teachers to build up your cup, bowl or vase, then fire, glaze and fire it again.

Studio 83; 13/F Winning Centre, 46–48 Wyndham Street; tel: 2523 3852; studio83. com.hk; Mon–Fri 11am–10pm, Sat 11am–8pm, Sun 11am–7pm; map E1
Sketch Studios; 4/F, Wai Lan House, 12 Lan Kwai Fong; tel: 5117 5092; www.sketch-studios.com.hk; Sun–Thu 5pm–11pm, private bookings daily 11am–9pm; map F1
The Pottery Workshop; Room 305, 3/F, Lyndhurst Building, 23–39 Lyndhurst Terrace; tel: 2525 7949; www.pottery workshop.com.cn; daily times vary; map E2

Tuck into flavoursome fare at a classic Cantonese teahouse

The Cantonese live to eat, and it is impossible to ignore the major role that food and everything around it plays in the lives of locals. A number of long-established Cantonese restaurants, with their no-nonsense decor and old-fashioned menus, are still going strong. A handful of these unpretentious places are referred to as teahouses; they serve hearty dim sum with tea from breakfast till late lunchtime, but they also have à la carte menus full of Cantonese classics. In contrast to the bright, plastic-looking, moderately priced local restaurant chains, teahouses offer dishes that have been house specials for years, served up by waiters who have long been part of the furniture.

An enduring favourite is **Lin Heung Tea House**, with its tall ceiling, strip neon lighting and tiled floor that does nothing to dull the sound of the animated dining room. The fare is tasty soups, seafood, poultry and meat dishes. Recommendations include bean curd, pork and vegetable soup; steamed razor clam with garlic; and braised aubergine with minced pork.

Heading into Central, **Yung Kee Restaurant** is famous for its roast meats: goose, duck, chicken and pork with rice and vegetables are a cut above many other kitchens – notice the constant takeaway queues. Decor here has been upgraded in recent years, and it's now pretty cosy.

Nearby, narrow multi-level **Luk Yu Teahouse** is most animated at lunchtime, when dim sum and other dishes can be enjoyed in wood-panelled comfort.

Lin Heung Tea House; 160–164 Wellington Street, Sheung Wan; tel: 2544 4556; map E3
Yung Kee Restaurant; 32–40 Wellington Street, Central; tel: 2522 1624; www.yungkee.com.hk; map F2
Luk Yu Teahouse; 24–26 Stanley Street, Central; tel: 2523 1970; map F2

Check out some of Soho and Noho's chic boutiques

As with the bar and restaurant scene in Soho, the Mid-Levels escalators led to the emergence of some interesting little shops, either visible from or very near the snaking metal staircase. An adjacent cluster of streets in Noho has seen a more recent gentrification, too. Few original businesses are left, as chic clothing and furniture shops nuzzle beside small cafés with tables on the pavement.

PMQ (35 Aberdeen Street; tel: 2870 2235; www.pmq.org.hk; map D3), once known as Hollywood Road Police Married Quarters, is a tastefully renovated low-rise residential block full of local independent fashion, accessory, craft collectives and gift shops representing small labels. With a handful of international restaurants and bars onsite, it makes for a pleasant two- or three-hour visit.

Button Hole (58 Peel Street; tel: 2899 2069; map D2) has an ever-changing stock of international fashion label overruns that are several rungs further up the chic ladder than the shops on Johnston Road in Wan Chai. Mostly womenswear and accessories, Chanel, Gucci and Alexander McQueen products and their like do crop up.

Chocolate Rain (67A Peel Street; tel: 2975 8318; www.chocolaterain. com; map D2) is one of a handful of jewellery and accessories shops in the vicinity. This one is particularly whimsical, with handmade bags, necklaces and other pieces coming together to tread a fine line between shop and art space.

One of Noho's eye-catchers is **Homeless** (29 Gough Street; tel: 2581 1880; www.homeless. hk; map D3), a lighting, furniture and homeware shop with quirky international stock, including plenty from Asia. It has a few other branches around town.

Free the flow of your vital energy – or qi – with a foot or body massage

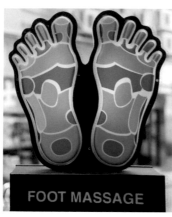

FOOT MASSAGE

Western health treatments abound in Hong Kong, but while here, it is worth trying things the Chinese way. Pressure-point massage techniques used by traditional practitioners in Hong Kong are a far cry from Western aromatherapy. If you see a sign displaying the sole of a foot, sometimes dissected with lines into labelled areas, with no English, chances are this is an acupressure centre. A traditional reflexologist will massage your feet to boost circulation and free the flow of the *qi*, or vital energy. Full-body treatments follow meridian points believed to run the length of the body. You can request how firmly you'd like to be massaged, but take as much

pressure as you can bear – the after-effects are worth it. Treatment can be carried out through clothing provided or through a sheet.

Establishments in Sheung Wan are clean, but can be spartan places with bright lights and curtained-off beds. Some have bilingual price lists for treatments; generally, expect to pay from HK$200 for a foot or neck and shoulder massage, and a bit more for a body massage.

Halite is a good example of the newer look that some of the traditional Chinese acupressure establishments are going for, with wooden floorboards and a more modern interior. It also offers Thai stretching massage and Western-style treatments – all at great value.

Foot Reflexology & Acupressure can be reached from the Sheung Wan end of Hollywood Road, and is a slightly plusher place. Some English is spoken, and tea or water is served first to allow you a few minutes' wind-down. The practitioners here know their pressure points.

Halite; Basement, CNT Commercial Building, 302 Queen's Road Central; tel: 2808 0028; map C3

Foot Reflexology & Acupressure; 8/F, Regent Centre, 88 Queen's Road Central; tel: 2997 7138; www.foothk.com; map F3

Stroll Sheung Wan and Western district's pungent streets of dried goods suppliers

Hong Kong merchants touting similar wares have a tendency to congregate cheek by jowl. In Kowloon, there are streets lined with pet shops or dedicated to sports shoe shops; and on both sides of the harbour the streets are filled with furniture-makers. For years, though, there has only been one neighbourhood devoted to dried foodstuffs and medicinal suppliers. Peddlers of these intriguing and pungent items crowd **Queen's Road West**, **Wing Lok Street**, and side streets off both, all the way west from Sheung Wan to Sai Ying Pun, just short of Kennedy Town. Walk along either and you'll see all manner of natural products being loaded and unloaded from lorries outside open shopfronts that are stacked with tubs and sacks of dried beans, seeds, mushrooms,

seafood and less familiar ingredients. They are used for traditional Chinese medicine (TCM), tonic drinks and in Cantonese cooking.

Interspersed between the larger traders are small TCM practitioners, who don't have far to go to replace stock; some have a pot or two of prescribed herbs simmering in earthenware pots, in preparation for customers.

Queen's Road West; map A4–B4
Wing Lok Street; map B5–C4

Unusual ingredients

It may surprise you to see the likes of dried sea horses and starfish displayed under glass – these have been prized medicinal and soup ingredients for centuries. In today's ecologically aware times, it may still be possible to spot a jarring ingredient or two: shark's fin being one.

Shop for silks, linens and handicrafts or have a drink in the handsome red-brick Western Market

Since few Hong Kong buildings with history have been spared the demolition ball, the striking **Western Market** building is a pleasure to behold. On a busy Sheung Wan street and right next to a pedestrian walkway that crosses multi-laned Connaught Road, this handsome red-brick colonial construction is a beacon of tasteful calm.

Built in 1906, it had become the worse for wear after some eight decades operating as a food market, but a series of renovations in the 1990s restored it to its former glory – though it was still little more than a hodgepodge of shops and stalls on the ground floor and upper level. Thankfully, a further makeover in 2003 brought back a sense of the building's market origins, with a string of quality fabric vendors selling everything from Chinese silk to Harris tweed – they moved here when the legendary 'Cloth Alley' bazaar on Wing On Street was closed down to make way for high-rise office towers. Prices are fair, and the merchants (who can also tailor) know their stuff.

Other arrivals included Cantonese restaurant **The Grand Stage** (tel: 2815 2311) upstairs, enlivened by afternoon 'tea dances', and **Das Gute** (tel: 2851 2872), a bakery and Western-style café on the ground floor.

Also downstairs are shops selling arts, crafts, jewellery, toys and some decent Hong Kong gifts and souvenirs. Shops and restaurants all keep different operating hours.

Western Market; 323 Des Voeux Road; www.westernmarket.com.hk; map C5

Get a taste of Asia at an authentic, no-frills Sheung Wan restaurant

While Soho has an abundance of stylish cosmopolitan restaurants, some more authentic, if less well dressed, ethnic establishments await in Sheung Wan.

Florinda Café is located inside the Macau ferry terminal, and while some dishes are fairly standard, the Macanese signatures in this restaurant are excellent. The presentation, a bit like the interior and the service, is no nonsense, but if you're not visiting Macau this is the place to try the dishes that evolved there under 450 years of Portuguese colonial rule. Good bets are the mildly spicy African chicken with rice, or the crispy pork chop bun and Portuguese egg tarts, which are justifiably popular.

Take your taste buds further afield at **Namaste Kitchen**, which serves up Nepalese and Indian cuisine in a cosy dining room. *Momos* (Nepalese dumplings with chicken or veggie fillings), breads, tandoori and curry dishes are all good.

Flavour and good value are hallmarks of **Viet Thai**. Starters of rice flour rolls are refreshing and packed with herbs; the pho – rice noodles with slivers of beef or shredded chicken in broths chock-full with fresh herb leaves and chopped spring onions – are also a good choice; Thai curries and fried noodles complete the picture. A brightly lit spot with brief service interventions, the food does the talking here.

Florinda Café; Shop 270–273, 2/F, Shun Tak Centre, 168–200 Connaught Road Central; tel: 2857 1933; map D5
Namaste Kitchen; 38 Queen's Road West; tel: 2795 7555; www.namastekitchen.com.hk; map B4
Viet Thai; 128 Connaught Road Central; tel: 2362 8663; map D4

Appease Buddhist deities at the Man Mo Temple

On the corner of Hollywood Road and Ladder Street is the wonderfully dark and atmospheric **Man Mo Temple**, built around 1842 on what must have been a little dirt track. Tourists regularly throng Man Mo, but this doesn't prevent regular worshippers visiting to fill the temple with thick smoke from their joss sticks. The immense incense spirals hanging from the ceiling can burn for weeks.

Man is the god of civil servants and of literature, and in Mandarin society, civil servants were the best-educated and most sophisticated group. Mo is the god of martial arts and war, and is more popularly known by his worshippers as Kuan Ti or Kuan Kung. Statues of the legendary Eight Immortals stand guard outside the temple; inside, two solid-brass deer (representing longevity) adorn the main chamber. Near the altar, there are two sedan chairs encased in glass. Years ago, when the icons of Man and Mo were paraded through Western on festival days, they were transported on these chairs.

Man Mo Temple; 126 Hollywood Road; tel: 2540 0350; www.man-mo-temple.hk; daily 8am–6pm; free; map C3

Street shrines

Street shrines are rare in Hong Kong these days, as unaccounted-for urban nooks are generally reclaimed as the city constantly develops. One or two still remain, though. Look for the shrine on the steps where Peel Street meets Wellington Street (map E3). Local devotees of earth god Pak Kung burn incense sticks and coils, and leave offerings of fruit.

Ride the world's longest series of covered escalators

Hong Kong can boast a few superlatives. It has the largest seated outdoor bronze Buddha in the world (at Po Lin Monastery, see page 150), the world's second most densely populated island (Ap Lei Chau, see page 140) and the world's longest series of covered escalators that zigzag their way halfway up The Peak. At some points the **Mid-Levels escalator** moves at street level; in other parts it soars high above it.

The escalator starts in Queen's Road Central and ends at Conduit Road in the pricey residential Mid-Levels neighbourhood. Its path through Soho accounts for the transformation of the area into one of the city's hippest zones. Canny restaurateurs and retailers realised in the early 1990s when it was built that they had a captive audience of well-heeled pedestrians to tempt with restaurants, cafés, bars and chic boutiques.

To catch a whole 23-minute leg of the escalator in one direction, you need to get your timing right. It was seemingly designed more for the convenience of the moneyed types who live in Mid-Levels, as it is in downhill-only mode for hillside commuters until 10am, travelling uphill after

that until midnight. A staircase runs parallel to the escalator, and is used by many people as a handy way to avoid crossing roads at street level.

The starting point that's easiest to find in Central is on Des Voeux Road, immediately above Central Market, where it connects with a covered walkway kitted out with timber and plants. It's definitely a useful way to get to Soho.

Mid-Levels escalator; map D1

Take the tram to its far western terminus – up-and-coming Kennedy Town, or stop en route at Sai Ying Pun

A few years before MTR stations opened in **Kennedy Town** and **Sai Ying Pun** (in 2014 and 2015 respectively), signs of gentrification had started creeping into these rough-cut neighbourhoods. Once fairly faceless residential and business areas with bustling shops and restaurants, the Island Line western extension, connecting these two neighbourhoods more quickly to the rest of Hong Kong, prompted plenty of new interesting cafés, restaurants, bars and shops to mushroom as apartment prices rose and a new breed of local and international resident moved in.

Take a tram rather than the underground train, which makes for a more chilled outing. It's about 10 minutes from Sheung Wan to Sai Ying Pun, and from there a further 15 minutes out to Kennedy Town.

Sai Ying Pun is home to dried seafood and herbal-medicine vendors on Queens Road West, but is now interspersed with places like **Okra**

Kitchen (no. 110; tel: 2806 1038; okra.kitchen), a Western chef's take on a buzzing Japanese isayaka bar. One of the best bars in this neighbourhood is **Ping Pong Gintoneria** (lower G/F, 129 Second Street; tel: 9835 5061; www.pingpong129.com); highlights include its quality, generously portioned Spanish-style G&Ts and wines. A snack menu is served in its tall-ceilinged basement.

In Kennedy Town, walk along the Praya, its waterfront path, where locals exercise in the morning and evening and watch cargo ships come and go from the nearby terminal. These parts are a laid-back alternative to Soho or Lan Kwai Fong, and again offer excellent international food and drink options.

Fresh tasty sushi and hot dishes at reasonable prices make up the menu at **Shin Shu Japanese** (Shop 5, 1 Davis Street; tel: 2872 0522). **Tequila on Davis** (1 Davis Street; tel: 2818 1766; tequilaondavis.com.hk) does what it says on the tin, complemented by casual Mexican fare. **Bistro du Vin** (1 Davis Street; tel: 2824 3010) cooks up the most elevated cuisine in the area under renowned chef Peter Teo. There's a very decent wine list too – all with a casual atmosphere.

Sai Ying Pun; map A5
Kennedy Town; map A5

Be spontaneous – fly to Macau by helicopter from Sheung Wan's Shun Tak Centre

If you fancy a spur-of-the-moment change of scene, you can make it happen within half an hour with a helicopter flight to Macau. Book a ticket on the third floor of the **Shun Tak Centre** in Sheung Wan. The flight itself is around 15 minutes, whisking you up through the towers of Hong Kong, westward above the Pearl River Estuary to the former Portuguese enclave and now Asia's Las Vegas.

Such express swiftness would depend on your timing for an available helicopter departure and, of course, you'd need to have your passport – Macau requires a separate visa (albeit free and stamped upon arrival). So do consider pre-booking. **Sky Shuttle Helicopters** leave every 30 minutes and more frequently at weekends; they start at 10.30am in Hong Kong, with the last one returning from Macau at 10.30pm.

Macau is definitely worthy of a day trip or overnight visit, with plenty of Portuguese buildings intact that date back more than four centuries. And there is also the lavish gaming side – this market opened to overseas operations several years ago, and big American and Australian casinos set up shop.

If you're not in such a hurry or wincing at the HK$4,300 one-way ticket price, you can take a high-speed ferry from the same building, which is also the Hong Kong to Macau ferry terminus; the journey takes just under an hour.

Sky Shuttle Helicopters; tel: 2108 9898; www.skyshuttlehk.com; map D5

WAN CHAI, CAUSEWAY BAY AND HAPPY VALLEY

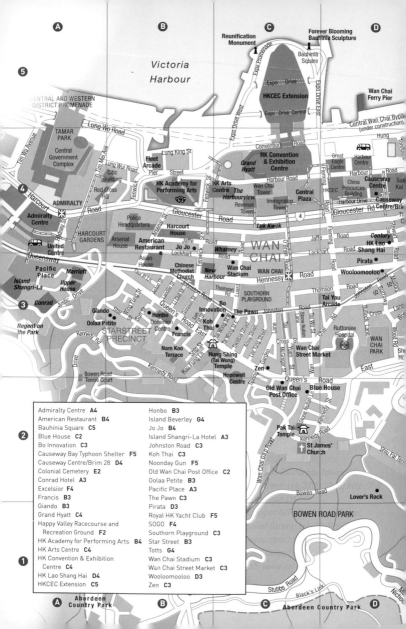

Victoria Harbour

Reunification Monument
Forever Blooming Bauhinia Sculpture

Bauhinia Square

HKCEC Extension

Wan Chai Ferry Pier

CENTRAL AND WESTERN DISTRICT PROMENADE

Central Wan Chai Bypass (under construction)

Lung Wo Road

TAMAR PARK

Central Government Complex

HK Convention & Exhibition Centre

Grand Hyatt

Great Eagle Centre

Harbour Centre

China Resources Building

Causeway Centre

Fleet Arcade Pier

HK Academy for Performing Arts

HK Arts Centre

The Harbourview

Wan Chai Tower

HKCEC

Harbour Drive

Causeway Centre/Brim

Citic Building

Red Cross HQ

ADMIRALTY

Admiralty Road

Admiralty Centre

HARCOURT GARDENS

United Queensway

Pacific Place

Marriott

Upper House

Island Shangri-La

Conrad

Regent on the Park

Gloucester Road

Police Headquarters

Harcourt House

American Restaurant

Asian House

Arsenal House

Jaffe Road

Jo Jo

Chinese Methodist Church

New Harbour

Wharney

Immigration Tower

Revenue Tower

Central Plaza

Luk Kwok

Gloucester Road

WAN CHAI

WAN CHAI

Hennessy Road

Jaffe Road

Lockhart Road

Century

HK Lao Shang Hai

Pirata

Wooloomooloo

Wan Chai Stadium

Johnston Road

SOUTHERN PLAYGROUND

Bo Innovation

The Pawn

Giando

Oolaa Petite

Honbo

Dominion Centre

Koh Thai

Francis

Tai Yau Arcade

STARSTREET PRECINCT

Nam Koo Terrace

Hung Shing (Tai Wong) Temple

Zen

Ruttonjee Hospital

WAN CHAI PARK

Wan Chai Street Market

Bowen Road Tennis Court

Kennedy Road

Hopewell Centre

Queen's Road

Old Wan Chai Post Office

Blue House

Pak Tai Temple

St James' Church

BOWEN ROAD PARK

Lover's Rock

Aberdeen Country Park

Aberdeen Country Park

Stubbs Road

Black's Link

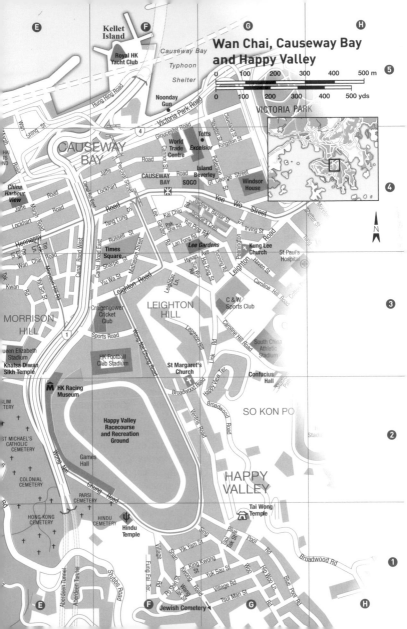

Wan Chai, Causeway Bay and Happy Valley

E   **F**   **G**   **H**

Kellet Island

Royal HK Yacht Club

Causeway Bay Typhoon Shelter

Noonday Gun

Hung Hing Road

Victoria Park Road

Gloucester Road

CAUSEWAY BAY

VICTORIA PARK

0   100   200   300   400   500 m

0   100   200   300   400   500 yds

World Trade Centre

Totts
Excelsior

Cleveland St
Yorkshire St
Kingston St
Gt George Street

Island Beverley
SOGO

Windsor House

CAUSEWAY BAY

Road

Yee   Wo   Street

China Harbour View

Jaffe   Road

Lockhart   Road

Percival Street

Cannon Street

Jardine's Bazaar St
Jardine's Cres
Pak Sha Rd
Yun Ping Rd

Irving St

Pennington

St Paul's Hospital

Hennessy   Road

Tang Lung

Russell St

Kai Chiu Rd
Lan Fong Rd
Lee Garden Rd

Lee Gardens

Hysan Ave

Kung Lee Church

Leighton Road

Caroline Hill Road

Wan Chai

Tin

Tai Yuen

Matheson Street

Canal Road West

Canal Road East

Times Square

Sharpe

Yiu Wa St

Leighton   Road

Leighton Ln

Lan Fong Rd

Haven Ave

C & W Sports Club

Caroline Hill Road

MORRISON HILL

Craigengower Cricket Club

Sports Road

LEIGHTON HILL

Leighton Hill

South China Athletic Stadium

Queen Elizabeth Stadium

Khalsa Diwan Sikh Temple

HK Football Club Stadium

St Margaret's Church

Broadwood Road

Confucius Hall

M HK Racing Museum

ST MICHAEL'S CATHOLIC CEMETERY

COLONIAL CEMETERY

HONG KONG CEMETERY

PARSI CEMETERY

HINDU CEMETERY

Hindu Temple

Happy Valley Racecourse and Recreation Ground

Games Hall

Chung   Road

Wong Nei Chung Road

Ventris Road

Broadwood Road

SO KON PO

HAPPY VALLEY

Tai Wong Temple

Aberdeen Tunnel

Stubbs Road

Fung Fai Tce

Village Rd

Shan Kwong Rd

Po Shan Rd

Sing   Woo

Tsui Man St

Yik Yam St
King Kwong St
Yuk Sau St
Village Road
Woo

Blue Pool Rd

Tak St

Hip Woo

Blue Pool Rd

Broadwood Rd

Jewish Cemetery ◄

E   **F**   **G**   **H**

5   **4**   **3**   **2**   **1**

N

Salute the ritual raising of the Hong Kong and China flags, then have breakfast

Start the day with a Hong Kong ritual. Members of the Hong Kong Police Force officially raise and lower the Hong Kong and China flags every morning at **Bauhinia Square**, next to the Convention Centre building.

The ceremony takes place at 7.50am daily, lasting just under 15 minutes, to a soundtrack of the People's Republic of China's national anthem. Officers are attired in regular uniform, which changes from winter to summer. On the first day of every month, they are accompanied by a rifle unit in ceremonial dress.

The ritual includes a rendition of the national anthem by the Police Band, followed by a bagpipe performance by the Police Pipe Band. On the second Sunday of each month, the ceremony is conducted by different youth groups.

Note the gold bauhinia statue, which represents Hong Kong's symbolic flower in bloom. Mainland Chinese visitors keenly snap photos of this and Reunification Monument, which bears inscriptions of the calligraphy of former President Jiang Zemin, who represented China at the Handover Ceremony in 1997.

While there, you can have breakfast at restaurants in the Convention Centre overlooking the square and harbour.

Bauhinia Square; Hong Kong Convention & Exhibition Centre; flag-raising daily 7.50am except in bad weather; map C5

Experience northern Chinese food in Wan Chai

Cantonese cuisine is everywhere in Hong Kong, and menus are pretty varied. However, it's possible to sample food from almost every other corner of China in the city's restaurants. Northern Chinese dishes from the region stretching from Shanghai to Beijing have long been popular with Hong Kong's local and international palates.

Now in its seventh decade, **American Restaurant** (known to many as the American Peking) took its name to attract US servicemen on R&R in Hong Kong. It is located at the quiet end of Lockhart Road, an area once peppered with girly bars – now only a few of them remain. English is understood here and the Northern Chinese menu presents an accessible choice of dishes, cooked to reliable stand-ards. Dishes include Shanghai's famous steamed *siu long bao* dumplings of minced pork; and from the Beijing region, Peking duck and seasoned sliced beef fried in small flat bread pockets are worthy signatures. The open dining room is cosily lit and tables spaced far enough apart for privacy.

Another Northern Chinese winner in the vicinity is **Hong Kong Lao Shang Hai Restaurant** in the Novo-tel Century Hotel. A non-Chinese reader might miss the large Chinese-character sign outside, with very small English wording. The *siu long bao* are good here, too, as are fresh, thick Shanghai noodles, fried with a sweetish soy sauce, chopped spring onion and your choice of meat: chicken, pork or beef. The interior and staff are quite dressed-up, but as at the American Peking, most diners are casually attired.

American Restaurant; 20 Lockhart Road; tel: 2527 7277; map B4

Hong Kong Lao Shang Hai Restaurant; upper G/F, Novotel Century Hotel, 238 Jaffe Road; tel: 2827 9339; map D4

Stimulate the senses with fresh exotic produce at Hong Kong's last remaining outdoor markets

Most of Hong Kong's fresh produce markets have been moved indoors, into charmless, utilitarian multi-storey buildings. Visit compact **Wan Chai Street Market**, near Admiralty and Wan Chai MTR stations, to see one of the few remaining collections of outdoor stalls.

If you're visiting the clothing outlet shops on Johnston Road (see page 79), about midway down you'll notice stalls poking out of Tai Yuen Street. This street runs down to Queens Road East; halfway along, it morphs from the cheap hosiery and kids' clothing stalls, with toy shops on both sides of the street, to vibrant fruit and vegetable stalls. Whatever is in season is displayed here – plus the imported permanent fixtures of bright pink dragon fruit, deep red lychees, oranges, mangoes and shiny red and green apples. Live seafood and meat are also sold, alongside sacks of rice and soy and other sauces. Dotted around the street market are small Thai grocery stores-cum-cafés, which primarily serve a small local community. Near the stalls are a few roast goose, duck and chicken speciality restaurants – easy to spot, as their prized ingredients hang prominently in the windows.

Still more produce is found in semi-hidden **Graham Street Market** in Soho, near Central MTR station. Here, as well as the typical selection of everyday Cantonese foodstuffs, is a smattering of flowers – all on a very small scale.

Both of these street markets were earmarked for demolition in recent years, but persistent and vocal public disapproval forced a government rethink. See them while you can.

Wan Chai Street Market; daily 7am–7pm; map C3
Graham Street Market; daily 7am–7pm; map page 50 D2–E3

Shoot a hoop or have fun with the family at Southorn Playground

In space-starved Hong Kong, very few strips of land remain undeveloped. Thankfully, the occasional park or tiny rest area breaks up the continual high-rises. Most districts also have indoor and outdoor sports areas, but these are often tucked away out of sight.

Southorn Playground is an exception. This recreational space lies between Hennessy and Johnston roads, slap in the centre of Wan Chai, and its marked basketball courts and hard-surface football pitch are in use day and night. Locals come here for a bit of exercise around a hoop or the goal-posts; join in the fun and land a few baskets or have a kick-about. There is also a children's playground.

If you are there on a floodlit weekday evening or at the weekend, there may well be a competitive league football game on. The crowd can get pretty animated and the atmosphere is friendly. At other times the benches in the stands are popular with retired Hong Kongers, who take hot drinks and snacks there to play board games and chat.

If you want to play a racquet sport, book a court at one of scores of government-run centres across Hong Kong. Search available ones at www.lcsd.gov.hk, where bookings and payments can be made; you can use your passport to register. It also lists public pools.

Southorn Playground; map C3

Kick back at an outdoor café or restaurant near the Wan Chai ferry pier

The Wan Chai ferry terminal, with its Star Ferry connection to Tsim Sha Tsui and Hung Hom in Kowloon, was something of a dead area several years ago. Despite being just off the waterfront, there were only a few unremarkable indoor restaurants without views.

Today, a clutch of places make for relaxed dining or a few drinks, and while not all have a view, all do have tables outside. Several are on the first floor of the **Causeway Centre and adjacent Brim 28** (both at 28 Harbour Road), rubbing shoulders with each other on a kind of elevated zigzagging dining piazza.

Frites (shop 6, Brim 28; tel: 2877 2422), as linguists may gather, is not short of deep-fried potato. It's the Belgian variety, rather than the French, mainly accompanying steak. But there's much more on offer here: salads, fish and poultry regularly crop up on the menu, often cooked using Asian sauces.

Up another notch in quality and price is **DiVino Patio Jack's Terrazza Ristorante** (shop 11; tel: 2877 3552). Its open kitchen – overlooking the terrace – is a hive of activity: bread is baked and cold cuts are sliced as a rotisserie turns. Buffet and set lunch is served daily, with à la carte listings at night; an early evening aperitivo brings complimentary Italian nibbles. Pizzas are popular here.

With the same view but from inside, three minutes west at the **Grand Hyatt** is the **Grand Café** (lobby level; tel: 2588 7722). Health-conscious items include the Grand Café 'superfood salad' with either sautéed shrimp or beef cubes, and steamed Alaskan toothfish fillet, with preserved vegetables, vinegar-soaked black beans, ginger and soy sauce, with steamed rice and Chinese soup.

Causeway Centre/Brim 28; 28 Harbour Road; map D4

Grand Hyatt; 1 Harbour Road; map C4

Root for designer bargains at Johnston Road's cut-price clothing outlets

Hong Kong Island and Kowloon used to have several areas where lucky browsers at clothing outlets might bag a designer label bargain from last season. Few remain now in Tsim Sha Tsui's Granville Road, but check out the 10 or so busy, open-fronted clothing stores in Wan Chai's **Johnston Road**.

Names such as **Sample King**, **Super Sample** and **Westwood** indicate you're in the right place; these joints take payment in cash only, and none has a telephone number. Devote some time to rooting

Johnston Road restaurants

In the same street as these cut-price outlets, the heritage building with colonial arched windows at no. 62 has been renovated to house a worthy restaurant with a bar attached. **The Pawn** (tel: 2866 3444; www.thepawn.com.hk; map C3), with a name reflecting the building's original incarnation as a pawn shop, serves modern British gastro-pub fare devised by respected UK chef Tom Aikens alongside dark beers. Try to bag one of the tables on the balcony. Next door at no. 60, on the first floor, is **Koh Thai** (tel: 3160 8535; www.koh thai.com.hk; map C3), a chilled indoor and terrace restaurant serving a good Thai menu, some with elevated touches – lobster pad thai anyone?

through the wares: clothes are hung on packed rails, and the cheapest items are piled into cardboard boxes that spill out onto the pavement or line long counters at the front of the shops. You may be surprised at the label bargains that pop up, including those made for UK, US and Australian department stores that don't have a retail presence in Hong Kong. Lesser-known brands of adult and kids' clothing are also on offer. Once you have trawled a few stores you may notice that the same items appear in two or three of the shops.
Johnston Road; map C3

Catch a show, film or exhibition at the Hong Kong Arts Centre

Be it Chinese or Western, the arts are a significant and growing part of the Hong Kong landscape – the amount of exhibitions, performances and arts festivals has doubled in the past two decades.

Opposite the waterfront, not far from the Wan Chai Ferry pier, the multi-purpose **Hong Kong Arts Centre** is a long-established champion of the arts. Fine art exhibitions, often cutting edge, are held here in an unusually spacious two-storey gallery space. Two theatres, including the intimate MacAuley Theatre, house various stage productions. There is a small cinema, and a local short-film festival is one of its annual highlights. You can also enjoy the harbour-view café and restaurant, and the bookshop.

Next door is the **Hong Kong Academy for Performing Arts**, where many of Hong Kong's singers and dancers are trained. In recent years its theatre has hosted a string of Australian productions of popular musicals, as well as family shows from the UK.

The cultural scene is set to surge again, with the forthcoming West Kowloon Cultural District in the construction stages.

Hong Kong Arts Centre; 2 Harbour Road; tel: 2582 0200; www.hkac.org.hk; map C4
Hong Kong Academy for Performing Arts; 1 Gloucester Road; tel: 2584 8500; www.hkapa.edu; map B4

Wine and dine the night away in trendy Star Street

In the late 1990s, regeneration hit the **Star Street** area of Wan Chai, which despite its address is a little closer to Admiralty. A cluster of low-rise car mechanics, workshops and flats were snapped up, and gleaming new towers appeared a few years later, with a couple of world-class restaurants at the ground level of gated luxury apartment blocks.

Giando (9 Star Street; tel: 2511 8912; www.giandorestaurant.com) is an upscale modern Italian in a warm wood and white-clothed interior that draws a well-heeled crowd. You'll pay a premium, but the pastas and risottos are phenomenal and it has a great wine list that includes boutique labels. An excellent brunch is served here. At the same address is **Oolaa Petite** (tel: 2529 38223; www.casteloconcepts.com/our-venues/oolaa-petite), the less formal sibling of Oolaa in Soho and serving good French brasserie fare in casual surroundings. Eat at bar tables by the open front or in the dining room.

The small roads off Star Street are also sprinkled with restaurants, bars and cafés. **Francis** (4–6 St Francis Street; tel: 3101 9521; www.francis.com.hk; map B3) brings some much needed authentic Middle Eastern cuisine to town. An Israeli chef cooks a small menu in this cosy establishment – there's a great set lunch and wines from Lebanon and Israel. Try the chicken schnitzel with za'atar and aioli.

Honbo (6–7 Sun Street; tel: 256708970; http://honbo.hk; map B3) serves good burgers (its name means hamburger in Cantonese), with ingredients sourced as locally as possible; its hamburger patties are 50 percent Hong Kong beef. Juicy fried chicken burgers get different treatment every couple of months – look out for the Korean version, with house kimchi and 'red dragon' sauce if it's on.

Star Street; map B3

Visit the charming Old Wan Chai Post Office, then walk the Green Trail

how they were a century ago. It is now an environmental resource centre, and visitors are welcome; it holds children's crafts courses, using recycled materials, on Sundays, and a small, peaceful garden houses models and information boards on renewable energy.

After admiring the listed building, climb the steep path behind it up to the **Wan Chai Green Trail** for a taste of sub-tropical foliage and a view over much of Hong Kong Island. The 1.5km (1-mile) trail is clearly marked and has information on the flora and fauna, before ending at Wan Chai Gap Park, where taxis and buses can return you to the city buzz.

Old Wan Chai Post Office; 221 Queen's Road East; tel: 2893 2856; Mon–Wed, Fri–Sun 9.30am–1pm, 2pm–5pm; map C2

Rampant redevelopment has meant that there are precious few bricks-and-mortar remnants of Hong Kong's past, but Wan Chai is one area where a few buildings recall earlier eras. The **Old Wan Chai Post Office** began life in 1912, serving as a police station for three years before becoming a post office – though it stopped operating as such in 1992, so don't expect to send a postcard. The counters, wood-beamed ceiling and wall of personal mailboxes have been restored to

The Blue House

One of the last surviving examples of a typically Hong Kong style of balconied tenement building, the **Blue House** (72–74A Stone Nullah Lane; tel: 2117 5843; map C2), is just around the corner from the Old Wan Chai Post Office. In 2007, in response to public outcry over demolition plans, this and eight other interconnected and nearby buildings constructed during the 1920s were saved and underwent renovation.

Taste the cuisines of South Asia's Grand Trunk Road amid the Lockhart Road buzz

Rightly regarded as a dining Mecca, Hong Kong is home to endless restaurants (more than 11,500 at last count). Most serve up regional Chinese dishes and pan-Asian menus, but you'll also find cuisines represented from all over the world. The long established Indian community means there are many excellent Indian restaurants; Western fare – think Italian, French and American-style steakhouses – has taken off in earnest since the mid-1990s; while Swiss, Burmese, Ukrainian and African restaurants are some of the more unusual finds here.

One Indian restaurant that was well ahead of the game is **JoJo**. Founded in 1985, it revamped in 2018 with a brighter interior boasting plenty of peacock blue and brass highlights, and a new focus for its menu. Dishes now draw on the Grand Trunk Road, which stretches from Chittagong in Bangladesh through to West Bengal and Delhi in India, Lahore and Peshwar in Pakistan and terminating in Kabul, Afghanistan. Age-old recipes are served à la carte; there's also a reasonably priced lunch buffet and weekend brunch.

Lockhart Road's former reputation as a go-go bar area gradually diminished as international restaurants, pubs and bars moved in. Of the sports bars here, **Wan Chai Stadium**, launched in 2018, is a winner, warmed with exposed brick walls and wooden flooring. Live international league football is the priority. Good quality casual dining counts steak and chips, barbecued ribs and cooked breakfasts as its menu signatures. And there's plenty of draft beer, wine and spirits behind the bar.

JoJo; 2/F, David House, 37–39 Lockhart Road; tel: 2527 3776; www.jojofood.com; map B4

Wan Chai Stadium; 72–86 Lockhart Road; tel: 3579 4466; www.wanchaistadium.com; map C3

Seek out some of Asia's sassiest clothing in Causeway Bay

Shoppers from all over Hong Kong flock to **Causeway Bay** for its Japanese department stores and scores of hip boutiques that stock international designer clothing, including lesser-known Japanese and Korean fashions.

The **Island Beverley** is the centre for cool threads and accessories shopping. An escalator whisks you from the street to the first few floors, where a labyrinth-like mall of narrow corridors circuits around tiny, trendy boutiques. It's mainly womenswear on sale here, with some gents' T-shirts and footwear. Although much is sourced from overseas, Island Beverley is also home to local fledgling designers.

Aimed at a late-twenties/early-thirties crowd, **Another Skin** (shop 129, 1/F; tel: 2469 9946) carries smart-casual women's quality clothing with personality sourced from Asia and beyond. **Little Fitting Room** (shop IB 229, 2/F) is another highlight, selling childrenswear items that lean towards the hip designs their parents might wear. Not many stores open before midday. The centre's higher floors are home to restaurants.

Just opposite the Island Beverley, iconic Japanese department store **SOGO** offers a massive selection of audiovisual equipment, clothing for all ages, suitcases, bags and just about anything you might need – everything is of pretty high quality. The basement has a good supermarket and fast-food outlets.

Behind SOGO, the Causeway Bay end of Lockhart Road has a string of fashionable local and Korean import boutiques.

Island Beverley; 1 Great George Street; www.islandbeverley.com.hk; map G4
SOGO; 555 Hennessy Road; tel: 2833 8338; www.sogo.com.hk; map F4

Hear the Noonday Gun sounded alongside Causeway Bay Typhoon Shelter

At the water's edge, one main road away from the dynamic heart of Causeway Bay, is **Causeway Bay Typhoon Shelter**, built to provide cover for the boats moored there. Live-aboard floating homes used to dock there until the early 1990s; now it's a parking spot for pleasure cruisers.

Right alongside the shelter is the **Noonday Gun**, site of possibly the last remaining colonial ritual in the territory. For the sake of tradition, despite the transfer of Hong Kong's sovereignty in 1997, an ex-British naval cannon is still fired as a time-check every day at noon.

A gun has been mounted here since the 1860s, but the idea preceded that: old British trading firm Jardines used a cannon to salute the arrival of company directors to their warehouse area on another part of Hong Kong Island. The Royal Navy took exception to this, believing such a mark of respect should be reserved only for top government officials, and consequently ordered Jardines to fire its gun as a daily time signal at noon as a form of punishment. Noel Coward immortalised the ritual in his 1930s song *Mad Dogs and Englishmen*.

At the other end of the typhoon shelter is the **Royal Yacht Club**, which can only be visited if you have reciprocal access through an overseas sailing club. Interestingly, this is the only Hong Kong organisation to have retained the 'Royal' moniker; after 1997 it disappeared voluntarily from other non-government establishment names.

Noonday Gun; 281 Gloucester Road; daily midday; free; map F5

Splash out on a sundowner or a meal with a million-dollar view

Victoria Harbour, framed by glitzy towers, is Hong Kong's quintessential backdrop, and a few restaurants and bars have both outdoor and indoor areas with spectacular harbour vistas.

In Causeway Bay at **The Excelsior** hotel, **Totts** is a restaurant and cocktail lounge with a killer panoramic view from its roof terrace. Tables next to its glass wall look out across the skyscraper-studded shore from Causeway Bay to Central. Enjoy a cocktail and mini kebabs from the bar menu; or a full Western meal out here or indoors.

In Wan Chai, also on a high floor with a glass-surrounded terrace and dining room, is Australian **Wooloomooloo Steakhouse**. It serves up great wines and cocktails perfect for a city sunset on its wood-decked outdoor area.

Also in Wan Chai and providing fabulous cityscape views, **Pirata** has a loyal following, particularly for its daily made fresh pasta. Its Italian menu spans far wider than this, and the cocktail and wine list keeps imbibers happy.

Totts; 34/F, The Excelsior, 281 Gloucester Road; tel: 2837 6786; www.mandarin oriental.com/excelsior/dining/totts; map G4
Wooloomooloo Steakhouse; 31/F, The Hennessy, 256 Hennessy Road; tel: 2893 6960; http://woo-steakhouse.com; map D3
Pirata; 29-30/F, 239 Hennessy Road; tel: 2887 0270; http://pirata.hk; map D3

Attend a floodlit evening race at Happy Valley

From September to July, there's a buzz in the air most Wednesdays on Hong Kong Island, as form guides and newspaper pundits are carefully studied ahead of the floodlit night races on turf at **Happy Valley Racecourse**. Built on reclaimed malaria-ridden marshland, Happy Valley first held races in 1846, and they proved an instant hit. Night racing was introduced here in 1973, and most visitors who attend say that this is one of the most enjoyable experiences of their time in Hong Kong.

Take a tram to Happy Valley or catch a taxi (ask your driver for a racing tip – you can then of course tip him to return the favour). Pay at the public entrance and take your place among the dynamic local punters. Million-dollar horses ridden by some of the world's best jockeys gallop past charged-up racing aficionados, designer-dressed tycoon couples and local residents all looking to win, and not shy to cheer their bet on.

Computerised betting, bilingual announcements and live broadcasting on enormous screens in the grounds makes it easy to follow and take part; designated tourist areas, staffed by customer relations assistants who can help explain how to place bets and answer other questions, make it even easier.

There are reasonably priced restaurants and bars to choose from. To heighten the experience, bring your passport and buy a tourist badge for access to the members' betting halls, trackside areas and members-only food and drink outlets. Or if you fancy privacy, hire a box.

The Sunday afternoon races at Sha Tin in the New Territories see even larger crowds, with far fewer tourists (see page 124).

Happy Valley Racecourse; Wong Nai Chung Road; tel: 1817; www.hkjc.com; evening races 7.15–9.15pm; map F2

KOWLOON

Kowloon

TSIM SHA TSUI

WEST KOWLOON
CULTURAL DISTRICT
(under construction)

Kun Yam Temple

Royal
Peninsula

Railway Approach

Hung Hom
KCR Station

Hong Kong
Coliseum

HUNG HOM

Cross Harbour
Tunnel

International
Mail Centre

KINGS PARK
RECREATION
GROUNDS

Club de
Recreio

Gun Club Hill
Barracks

India
Club

HK Museum
of History

HK Science
Museum

South Seas
Centre

Empire Centre

Regal
Kowloon

Energy
Plaza

CENTENARY
GARDEN

Royal
Garden

Kowloon
Ctr

Tsim Sha
Tsui Centre

Avenue of Stars

Deck n Beer

South
Kowloon
Magistracy

Rosary
Church

DNA

Peninsula
Hotel

Hilton
Towers

Houston
Ctr

Shangri-La

Mirror
Tower

Wing On
Plaza

EAST TSIM
SHA TSUI

Avenue
of Stars

New World
Centre

Inter-
Continental

Mabu

Kowloon
Union
Church

HK
Observatory

All Night
Long

Rise
Commercial
Building

Braemar
Hill

Inter-Continental

SIGNAL HILL
GARDEN

Oyster &
Wine Bar

The Sheraton

HK Museum of Art

JORDAN
Kowloon
Prudential
Centre

Cox's Road

The One

Sim's
TST

K11

Chungking
Mansions

The Peninsula

Yue Hwa

St Andrew's
Church

(Golden Mile)

Heritage
Discovery
Centre

KOWLOON
PARK

CHINESE
GARDEN

Nathan Road

(Golden Mile)

Ned Kelly's
Last Stand

Hutong Peking

HK Space
Museum

HK Cultural
Centre

Chinese Arts
& Crafts

Royal
Pacific

ORNAMENTAL
GARDEN

Kowloon
Park Drive

Tang Court

The Langham

Aqua Spirit

Hullett House/
Heritage 1881

Clock
Tower

Ste Ferry
Pier

China
Hong Kong City

China Ferry
Terminal

Marco Polo
Prince

Marco Polo
Gateway

Canton Road

Harbour
City

Star
House

Ocean
Terminal

Lin Cheung Rd

Lin Cheung Road

The Waterfront

Elements

International
Commerce Centre (ICC)

Kowloon
Station

Union
Square
KOWLOON

Jordan
Road

AUSTIN

Government
Offices

Austin Road
West

0   100   200   300   400   500 yds
0   100   200   300   400   500 m

Take tea in TST – with scones or dim sum

One of the best pleasures of a visit to Hong Kong is to take a break from the clamour of streets and shops and relax with a steaming cup of freshly brewed tea. Spoil yourself in a refined refuge in Tsim Sha Tsui (TST) and take tea the English or the Cantonese way.

Warm, oven-fresh scones and finger sandwiches await in **The Lobby** at **The Peninsula** hotel (Salisbury Road; tel: 2696 6772; hongkong. peninsula.com; daily 2–6pm; map C1), which serves traditional English afternoon tea. Note that advance booking is not possible. Next door at **1881 Heritage**, another top-notch afternoon tea is served in **Heritage Parlour** (1/F, Hullet House, 2A Canton Road; tel: 3988 0101; daily 2.30–5.30pm; map B1), which can be had on its harbour-facing balcony.

The Cantonese term *yum cha* literally means 'drink tea', but it

The Murray

On the other side of the harbour in Central, the city's newest heritage hotel, **The Murray** (22 Cotton Tree Drive; tel: 3141 8888; daily 2.30–5.30pm), also serves a fine afternoon tea – with elegant china and an interesting house tea and coffee blends – in its sleek Garden Lounge.

also refers to the enjoyment of a tea-fuelled dim sum meal. Two of the most refined places for *yum cha* are at **Spring Moon** in The Peninsula, a take on a Shanghai teahouse with fine dim sum and a 'tea master' who explains the differences between 29 varieties; and imperial-looking **Shang Palace** (Basement, Kowloon Shangri-La, 64 Mody Road; tel 2733 8754; map D2), where 10 premium teas are brewed with a monthly changing dim sum list.

Shop at a space-age mall in contemporary Kowloon

In recent years, Kowloon's neighbourhoods of Jordan and Tsim Sha Tsui have seen the arrival of some futuristic mall complexes with a wider variety of brands than most older shopping centres.

Elements, atop Kowloon MTR and Airport Express stations, is one of the most spacious. Its wide corridors, displaying modern sculpture, are very easy on the eye. International fashion and sports brands, high-end home accessories and electronics stores are all housed here. Head up to its podium-level bars and cafés, where tables spill onto a piazza-like terrace bordered with potted greenery. For the adventurous or those with kids in tow, there is an ice rink on the ground floor.

The edgiest malls on the block, on either side of Nathan Road in Tsim Sha Tsui, are **K11** and **i-Square**. Both reflect the cyber age in their design, with lots of white space and projected lights. K11's standout stores include **Matter Matters** (level 1, tel: 3122 4049), which offers home-grown youthful, tasteful fashion and accessories for both genders; and local chic men's fashion brand **Son of a King** (level 1, tel: 6884 4877), with its appealing mix-and-match range. Restaurants are thoughtfully stacked at one end

of the mall in a 'gourmet tower'.

i-Square is even more stark and minimal, aimed at a young adult shopper – designer streetwear, bags and accessories feature in abundance. **Radar Audio Company** (shop 505, tel: 2327 8861) is a branch of the high-end audio equipment specialist that's enjoyed a good reputation in Hong Kong since the 1980s. **New Balance** (shop 404, tel: 2947 9182) has limited-edition footwear and clothing. There are several cafés and noodle bars; for a more indulgent meal hit the upper floors. One of Hong Kong's best cinemas, **UA**, with its IMAX screen, is on the seventh floor.

Elements; 1 Austin Road West; tel: 2735 5234; www.elementshk.com; map A3
K11; 18 Hanoi Road; tel: 3118 8070; http://hk.k11.com; map C2
iSquare; 63 Nathan Road; tel: 3665 3333; www.isquare.hk; map C2

Absorb the detail of ancient Chinese and colonial-era paintings at the Hong Kong Museum of Art

The **Hong Kong Museum of Art** on the Kowloon waterfront is a great place to while away a few hours. Not only does it house some of the world's finest examples of ancient Chinese art, but it also contains hundreds of traditional and contemporary works. It is currently undergoing a thorough, modernising renovation and is scheduled to reopen in 2019.

Among the most fascinating artworks are a number of China Coast pieces by British-born George Chinnery (1774–1852), as well as works by several of his peers. The paintings show a 19th-century Hong Kong, Macau and Southern China far removed from their modern-day appearances, at a time when South China ports were in transition from fishing villages to trading hubs. Chinnery, who also spent time in India, painted in oil on canvas in meticulous detail.

Much of this kind of artwork at the museum is rotated, so you never know exactly what will be on show; but you might also see old engravings from British periodicals, which illustrated articles on the region in the days before photography.

Traditional Chinese art, antiquities and jewellery remain on permanent display. Nomadic pieces caricature animal motifs, such as wild cats and wolves – revered and feared on the desolate plains. Antique accessories include elaborate long court necklaces of semi-precious stone and noblewomen's headdresses. The Gold section features ornaments and jewellery that span Chinese dynasties and provinces alike.

The Xubaizhai Collection of prized examples of Chinese ink painting and calligraphy on both silk and paper is a house treasure; some works date back as far as the 15th century, yet are immaculately preserved.

Contemporary Hong Kong art is also exhibited here, with themed exhibitions regularly presenting mixed and new media. The museum shop is one of the best places to look for art books and prints in Hong Kong.

TST MUSEUMS

Tsim Sha Tsui (TST) is the prime place in Hong Kong to visit for a museum fix; all are government-run and details can be found at www.lcsd.gov.hk/ce/museum. The **Hong Kong Museum of History** (100 Chatham Road South; tel: 2724 9042; hk.history.museum; map D3) has an attractive collection of natural, local and ethnic history exhibits – with plenty of vintage film footage in screening rooms. Next door, the **Science Museum** (2 Science Museum Road; tel: 2732 3232; hk.science.museum; map D3) has over 500 exhibits on permanent display in 18 galleries, including robotics, computers, phones and a miniature submarine, and is a popular spot for families and kids. The **Space Museum** (10 Salisbury Road; tel: 2721 0226; www.lcsd.gov.hk/CE/Museum/Space; map C1), another kiddie fave with its unmissable planetarium dome next to the Museum of Art, screens astronomical and natural-history documentaries, some in OMNIMAX Sensaround format. Its displays include interactive scale-model rockets and genuine astronaut suits.

Hong Kong Museum of Art; 10 Salisbury Road; tel: 2721 0116; http://hk.art.museum; check website for hours; charge; map C1

Begin a Tsim Sha Tsui bar crawl in buzzing Knutsford Terrace

Knutsford Terrace, a discreet pedestrianised stretch, is one of the most popular places in Kowloon for alfresco dining, drinking and socialising. Come here to get your TST bar crawl off to a swinging start.

Assembly (no. 6; tel: 2723 6588; map C3) is a popular restaurant-cum-bar establishment. The cocktail, wine, spirit and beer list here is enormous, with happy hour daily except Saturdays – its good tapas menu helps balance the act. For a party crowd and a lively live band, **All Night Long** (no. 9; tel: 2367 9487; map C3) does the job.

If big band jazz music is your thing, move on for a drink at **Ned Kelly's Last Stand** (11a Ashley Road; tel: 2376 0562; map B2), where long-serving musicians get things going after 9pm.

Deserve a splurge? Across the road from Knutsford Terrace is **Vibes** bar at **The Mira** hotel (118–130 Nathan Road; tel: 2315 5599; www.themirahotel.com; map C2), a leafy courtyard terrace lounge with top cocktails – notably those using craft gins. A gourmet snack menu rounds things off.

Perched at the top of **The Peninsula** hotel on Salisbury Road (map C1), with an interior by Philippe Starck, **Felix** (28/F; tel: 2366 6251) has two enclosed bar areas – one quiet, one buzzing. Pull up a Starck stool at its light-box-like Long Table to take in the proceedings against a Hong Kong harbour backdrop. Bar snacks here are particularly tempting, and the restaurant's à la carte menu can also be ordered at either bar.

Browse a lively outdoor market for an affordable Hong Kong souvenir

Much outdoor trading in Hong Kong has moved indoors over the past decade or so, but a few remaining Kowloon outdoor markets are fun to browse.

Jade Market in Yau Ma Tei gets its fair share of tourists, but is also a local favourite for jade and other semiprecious stone jewellery. For thousands of years, jade has been associated with long life, good health and good fortune by the Chinese. Pendants, bracelets, rings and brooches in various hues are the main finds here. Traders are generally reputable – if a price is very cheap, presume it is very low-grade or not real jade.

Ladies' Market in Mong Kok is another consumer hotspot. As its name indicates, most items on sale are for women: clothing, bags, accessories and cosmetics make up the bulk of the stock. But kids' clothes, toys and household gear can all be had, at good prices.

Over in Jordan, the market most visited by tourists is **Temple Street Market**, and for good reason: if looking for a souvenir or present, it is hard to walk away empty-handed. Chinese-style costumes for children, T-shirts, funky watches and clocks, chopsticks sets and ornaments are all up for grabs. There are scores of restaurants around the market, and fortune-tellers reading palms and faces; and with an audio backdrop provided by a few remaining CD and DVD stalls, it's a pretty lively scene.

Jade Market; Kansu and Battery Streets; daily 11am–6pm; map B4
Ladies' Market; Tung Choi Street; daily midday–11.30pm; map C6
Temple Street Market; daily 4pm–midnight; map B5

Go for an after-dinner stroll along the harbour promenade, and delight in the Symphony of Lights

The best unobstructed view of Hong Kong Island can be seen from the very tip of the Kowloon Peninsula, where a wide pedestrian walkway stretches from TST's Star Ferry all the way to Hung Hom Station.

At 8pm nightly, the **Symphony of Lights** illuminates towers and the night sky on both sides of the water with LED and laser lighting effects. The best vista is from the upper viewing deck of the promenade – a raised platform with a line of benches in front of the Hong Kong Cultural Centre. If you left your tripod at home, a handful of digital image-making stalls offer reasonably priced prints.

Although more intense at night, the view is also striking by day. East of the Cultural Centre, beyond the InterContinental Hotel and New World Centre, the **Avenue of Stars** – think handprints in cement, à la Beverly Hills – can be seen more clearly at daytime, too. Film fans should look out for prints and plaques honouring Jackie Chan, Chow Yun-Fat, Jet Li and John Woo among others, as well as a bronze sculpture of Bruce Lee.

Waterfront promenade; map B1–E2

Tableside views

One café-bar with outdoor tables for harbour-side refreshment – where you can actually hear the sound of the swell and passing vessels – is **Deck n Beer** (Salisbury Road; tel: 2723 9227; map C1), a relaxed people-watching spot with wooden decking. For a wider aerial perspective on the nightly light show, with quality international fare served in casual surroundings, there's **Wooloomooloo Prime** (Level 21, The One, 100 Nathan Road; tel: 2870 0087; www.woo-prime.com; map C2).

Get fitted up for a bargain price in Tsim Sha Tsui

If you are more accustomed to buying clothes off the peg, Hong Kong makes it affordable to treat yourself to a perfect fit. Bespoke bargains are to be had across **Tsim Sha Tsui** at dozens of small tailors' workshops. Chinese and Indian tailors have honed these skills over generations, and their deft cutting and needlework, in the style and material of your choice, offer true value for money.

Usefully, or annoyingly, depending on whether or not you are in the market for a made-to-measure suit, shirt, dress or the like, street touts in this neighbourhood routinely approach those they presume are tourists. Don't feel obliged to listen to the sales patter – if interested, cut to the chase and ask for prices of individual garments or a package. Of course, for a true picture of what to expect, visit the tailor to inspect samples of their work.

Testimonial letters from satisfied customers are routinely displayed – nowhere more so than at **Sam's Tailor**, where suits and dresses have been run up for many a Western and Asian celebrity.

Beware of misleading tailor touts, though; remember to check costs and materials used. Suits and dresses can be turned around in 24 hours, but allow more time if you can, as it is wise to suggest two fittings (after the initial measuring-up) before you pick up the final garment (or have it delivered to your hotel, usually at no extra charge if you're staying in or near the neighbourhood).

Sam's Tailor; G/F, Burlington Arcade, 90–94C Nathan Road; tel: 2367 9423; www.samstailor.com; map C2

Find peace in the landscaped grounds of two urban temple complexes

In the heart of bustling Kowloon are two tranquil urban oases: **Wong Tai Sin Temple** and **Chi Lin Nunnery**.

You will know you have arrived at the Wong Tai Sin Temple when you hear the sound of rattling *chim*, the bamboo sticks used for fortune-telling. Known as 'the fortune-tellers' temple', this Taoist temple complex in a natural setting at the heart of urban Kowloon is the liveliest and most colourful place of worship in Hong Kong. Constantly bustling with worshippers, it is certainly one of the most rewarding for outsiders to visit. The carvings on the rear of the main altar depict the story of the god Wong Tai Sin, a simple shepherd who is said to have been given the formula for an elixir for immortality by a heavenly spirit. There is a small entrance charge to some areas, such as the lovely **Good Wish Garden** (though this is not always open).

Flanked by a lily pond and instantly recognisable by its beautifully embellished carved wooden roofs, the huge Buddhist Chi Lin complex was built between the 1930s and 1990s, but entirely in the classic style of the Tang dynasty (AD 618–907). Its seven wooden halls were even constructed using wooden tenons instead of nails. Nestled among the surrounding high-rise apartment blocks is the tranquil **Nan Lian Garden**, a relatively new public park also built in the Tang style. The scenic garden is meticulously landscaped over 3.5 hectares (8.5 acres), in which every hill, rock, body of water, plant and timber structure has been placed according to specific rules and methods.

Wong Tai Sin Temple; 2 Chuk Yuen Village; tel: 2327 8141; www.siksikyuen.org.hk; daily 7am–5pm; free; map C8
Chi Lin Nunnery; 60 Fung Tak Road, Diamond Hill; tel: 3658 9366; www.nanlian garden.org; daily 7am–9pm; free; map E5

Treat yourself to a gourmet feast at a top international restaurant or try the creations of a local three-star chef

Celebrity chefs from overseas have been a big hit in town in recent years, and two of them have set up home under the same hotel roof at the InterContinental Hong Kong, overlooking the harbour.

Rech by Alain Ducasse (lobby level; tel: 2721 1211), flying the flag for the global empire of the big-name French chef, launched in 2017, taking over from what was Spoon restaurant. The seafood restaurant has been a winner with Hong Kongers, for whom quality marine produce is a firm favourite. Dishes are superb, presented with modern French flair. Polite, attentive service in a relaxed, stylish environment with a feeling that you're perched right on the edge of the harbour. What's not to like?

Nobu (2/F; tel: 2721 2323), headed up by king of Japanese fusion Nobu Matsuhisa, houses a more elegant dining room in its Hong Kong branch than some elsewhere. The menu concept, though, is constant: contemporary Japanese with South American accents, reflecting the years Matsuhisa spent in Peru.

He may not be a globally known name, but head chef Kwong Wai-keung of **T'ang Court** at The Langham in Tsim Sha Tsui is esteemed by local gourmands and visiting foodies alike. Cantonese dishes here have fabulous depth and the whole dining experience merited three stars in the eyes of the Michelin guide (2017).

Rech and Nobu; InterContinental Hong Kong, 8 Peking Road; tel: 2313 2323; www.hongkong-ic.intercontinental.com; map C1

T'ang Court; 1/F and 2/F, The Langham Hong Kong, 118–130 Nathan Road; tel: 2132 7898; www.langhamhotels.com/en/the-langham/hong-kong/dining/tang-court; map B2

Snap up top-quality items from Mainland China at these department stores

Some of Mainland China's best clothing, artwork and foodstuffs are shipped south to Hong Kong, and many visitors track down an item or two from the big country north of the border to take home.

Small tourist shops and some market stalls offer plenty of keepsakes, but for products that will last and whose quality will be more appreciated, there are a couple of reputable department stores worth investigating.

For silk clothing, household porcelain, tea, medicinal herbs and other top-grade products from Mainland China, **Yue Hwa's** flagship store in Jordan is the best bet. You'll find linen tablecloths and sheets; casual and smart clothing, with Western cuts but made by some of the top Chinese brands, also feature. The art section sells paintings and prints, sculptures and religious statues.

In Tsim Sha Tsui, **Chinese Arts & Crafts** has less homeware and only top-end clothing. It focuses on fine ornaments and jewellery: elaborate carvings of jade, crystal and other semiprecious stones are displayed on pedestals. One large jade piece, depicting the mythical nine dragons after which Kowloon is named, is priced at HK$8.8 million.

Both stores have other branches across Hong Kong.

Yue Hwa; 301–309 Nathan Road, Jordan; tel: 3511 2222; www.yuehwa.com; daily 10am–10pm; map C4

Chinese Arts & Crafts; Shop no.1, G/F China Hong Kong City, 33 Canton Road, Tsim Sha Tsui; tel: 2735 4061; www.chineseartsandcrafts.com.hk; daily 10.30am–7.30pm; map B2

Peruse cutting-edge artwork in Kowloon's specially converted creative spaces

Contemporary fine art has seen something of a renaissance in Hong Kong. With the help of government grants, two disused industrial premises have been converted into arts spaces.

Cattle Depot Artist Village, in a scruffier part of East Kowloon, began life in 1997, when it was renovated from a slaughterhouse to workshops and galleries. Artistically inclined non-profit tenants were granted space, and visitors are welcome to visit their galleries. Art group **Artist Commune** (tel: 2104 3322) is one organisation that settled there, building studios, holding exhibitions and events and inviting international talent to its artist-in-residency programme. Another group, **1a Space** (tel: 2529 0087; www.oneaspace.org. hk), has carved out a reputation as a leader of Hong Kong's contemporary visual arts scene, organising activities and exhibitions, and producing publications. **Videotage** (tel: 257301869; videotage.org.hk) merges the concepts of video and montage, focusing on the development of video and new media art. It has held cutting-edge audiovisual exhibitions and performances.

In 2008, a larger converted factory space opened: the **Jockey Club Creative Arts Centre**, in Shek Kip

Mei. The workshops of some 150 local artists, performance groups and musicians can be visited, and it has a café. There is plenty to see at JCCAC – workshops for school children, plays in rehearsal and art taking shape in studios. **Hong Kong Open Printshop** (Room 5, 8/F; tel: 2319 1660; www.open-printshop. org.hk) is one of the territory's few printmaking facilities. **The Hong Kong Puppet and Shadow Art Center** (Room 6, 13/F; tel: 3165 0958; www.hkpsac.org) teaches string and Asian silhouette puppet-making, and rehearses performances here.

Cattle Depot Artist Village; 63 Ma Tau Kok Road; Wed–Sun 10am–10pm; free; map E5
Jockey Club Creative Arts Centre, 30 Pak Tin Street; tel: 2353 1311; www.jccac.org. hk; daily 10am–10pm; free; map B8

Get a bird's-eye view over Hong Kong while savouring an exquisite meal or cocktail

Combining a fine meal with an elevated harbour panorama is a treat that any visitor to Hong Kong should try to lavish on themselves. If a full meal is beyond budget, most of these glamorous rec-ommendations – all in Tsim Sha Tsui – have bar areas, where the backdrop can be enjoyed over a cocktail or two. From up here, you get a sense of how narrow most of Kowloon's streets really are – and how the pavements teem with ant-like Hong Kongers.

Aqua Spirit (30/F; One Peking Road; tel: 3427 2288; www.aqua. com.hk; map B1) is one such example. Theatrically dark to make the most of the 360-degree views of Victoria Harbour and Kowloon, it sits atop Aqua restaurant, where the menu is split into Italian and Japanese cuisine. Weekend brunch is a relaxed time to soak up the view. Book in advance for semi-private booths. The bar can be booked for a minimum charge, which walk-in visitors don't incur.

One floor down in the same building, **Hutong** restaurant (28/F, One Peking Road; tel: 3428 8342; www.aqua.com.hk) is another good spot for the nightly harbour light show at 8pm (see page 98). Here, Northern Chinese food is served in a dark contemporary-meets-antique environment.

Oyster & Wine Bar (18/F, Sheraton Hong Kong Hotel & Towers, 20 Nathan Road; tel: 2369 1111 ext 3145; www.sheratonhongkong hotel.com/oysterandwinebar; map C1) has a sophisticated yet understated ambience that lets the view do the talking and oozes 'special occasion'. Its reputable fresh oyster bar selection is joined by an always-impressive Western fine-dining menu; signatures include crab cakes and grilled Atlantic sea bass. There is a separate bar serving a top-tier snack menu. The Sunday champagne brunch is a good way to enjoy the impressive view by day.

Philippe Starck-designed restaurant and bar **Felix** (see page 96) offers another view from on high, from within a notable interior. **Wooloomooloo Prime** (see page 98) is yet another good option.

For an eye-in-the-sky splurge in a helicopter, **Heliservices**, in con-junction with The Peninsula hotel, offers some **Fly and Dine** packages (http://hongkong.peninsula.com/en/special-offers/fly-and-dine), available daily, which combine a 15-minute helicopter ride from the hotel's rooftop, plus a meal in one of its restaurants. Prices vary according to the flights and meals selected and the number of people taking part.

The best viewing platform in town

Sky 100, on the 100th-floor viewing area in the **International Commerce Centre** (ICC) tower in West Kowloon (1 Austin Road West; tel: 2613 3888; sky100.com.hk; Sun–Thu 10am–9pm, Fri–Sat 10am–10.30pm; charge; map A3), brings panoramas previously unseen in Hong Kong. Not only is it scores of floors higher than any other, but most developers have previously been too concerned with rental yield to consider such a thing.

The skyscraper's roof stands at 484 metres (1588ft), and is the third tallest in the world. A café here is run by the Ritz-Carlton, Hong Kong, the hotel on the uppermost 15 floors of the ICC, which became the world's tallest hotel in 2010 – and there are great views from its restaurants and rooftop **Ozone Bar** (tel: 2263 2270).

Enter a warren of boutiques with attitude

Around the Chatham Road end of Granville Road is a cluster of small, hip boutiques. The pioneer was the Beverley Commercial Building, Hong Kong's first shopping arcade catering for young hipsters, but in the last few years it has become overrun with other businesses and the mantle has been passed to **Rise Commercial Building** – a veritable warren of fashionable outlets.

Lots of the alternative fashion and lifestyle products found here are designed by young Hong Kongers. Many shops also display unique pieces that have been sourced from around Asia or beyond. Japanese and Korean clothing and footwear have been popular with the fashion-conscious for some time here. Among others, **Houses shop** (no. G22–24; www.housesshop.com.hk) stocks a variety of accessories and grooming products for the dapper gent. **Dusty** (no. 133; www.dusty.com.hk) offers wacky and stylish watches.

Near Rise Commercial Building, newer **DNA Galleria** mall is chock full of trendy shops. In addition to the official main entrance address, there is also an entrance on Granville Circuit. **Made by Kawai** (no. 21) sells Korean street wear and some self-painted fashion accessories and jewellery.

The side streets around here have plenty of interesting small outlets too, displaying an ever-changing assortment of clothes, accessories and costume jewellery. In this vicinity, many places open shop around mid-afternoon and stay trading until late.

Rise Commercial Building; 5–11 Granville Circle; map C2
DNA Galleria; 61–65 Chatham Road South; map C2

Take a neon sign tour along and around Kowloon's 'Golden Mile'

A century ago, Kowloon Peninsula's main artery, **Nathan Road**, was tree-lined and elegant, and its low-rise buildings were desirable residences. But since the 1960s, it has become known for the stretch of large-scale neon signage that overhangs the road and inspired its nickname, 'The Golden Mile'. It is still a spectacle today.

Stand at the end of Nathan Road in Tsim Sha Tsui. You are now looking due north along Kowloon's main artery, ablaze with colourful signs. **Big Bus Tours** (tel: 2723 2108; www.bigbustours.com) ply the route, but exploring on foot allows you to deviate onto side streets like Peking and Haiphong roads, neck craned upwards at the festival of lights. If pushed for time, walk up Nathan Road to the junction with Jordan Road, then look left – this takes no more than 15 minutes, and the orgy of neon on both streets is quite a sight.

Most signs are in Chinese characters only, and a large portion advertise Cantonese restaurants or jewellery shops. One much-repeated sign is a circle crowned by what looks like bat wings – this is the time-honoured motif for pawn shops.

Nathan Road; map C1–C3

Cross the harbour on Hong Kong's quintessential form of transport, the Star Ferry

From Rolls-Royce to rickshaw, Hong Kong offers every mode of conveyance. But the territory's quintessential form of transport is the Star Ferry. Shunting back and forth across Victoria Harbour between Tsim Sha Tsui and Central piers, these green-and-white ferries link the community together in a way that is both symbolic and practical.

The dozen-strong fleet would win few prizes for glamorous design. Yet the clanking gangways, weather-beaten coxswains and solid wooden decks have a timeless character and the five-minute crossing provides views that are second to none – particularly at twilight. The upper decks avoid engine-room noise and fumes.

The first of the current 'Star' fleet made their maiden voyages in 1898. Until Hong Kong Island was connected to Kowloon by road tunnel and the MTR in the 1970s, the Star Ferry was the prime way to cross the harbour – these days it is generally quicker to use the MTR.

Star Ferry also runs routes from Tsim Sha Tsui to Wan Chai on Hong Kong Island – check the website.

Around the Tsim Sha Tsui piers are a number of operators who offer harbour cruise packages by day or night, including **Watertours of Hong Kong** (tel: 2926 3868; www.water tours.com.hk). For something a little more upmarket, you might jump aboard red-sailed wooden junk **Aqua Luna** (tel: 2116 8821; www. aqua.com.hk), which offers daytime and evening cocktail cruises, sometimes with live musicians aboard. *Star Ferry; tel: 2367 7065; www.star ferry.com.hk; daily 6.30am–11.30pm; map B1 and page 26 F5*

Observe small-scale pets and their owners at Bird Garden and 'Fish Street'

Although pet dogs have become a little more popular in the last few years, in space-challenged Hong Kong smaller domestic companions – if any – are preferred. Caged birds have been popular with retirees for generations; many take their winged friends to meet other owners in parks or teahouses that permit them. Pet fish are traditionally thought to impart good energy in a home; some believe that when a fish dies, it absorbs the bad luck that would otherwise have fallen on a person living there.

Hong Kong has themed streets across its various districts, and Mong Kok is the go-to area for pet birds and fish. Following the outbreaks of avian flu, the old 'Bird Street' that traded in feathered pets was ordered to cease its function. In its place came the **Yuen Po Street Bird Garden**, which functions similarly but is regulated for hygiene. It is the favoured gathering place of Hong Kong's songbird owners, with some 70 stalls selling birds and bird-keeping paraphernalia.

Tung Choi Street is packed with goldfish, tropical fish, turtles, aquariums and everything for your aquatic pet needs. Shops open from around 10.30am until 10pm, and the area is popular with local families and kids.

Yuen Po Street Bird Garden; www.bird-garden.hk; daily 7am–8pm, map C8
Tung Choi Street; map B7

People-watch at dynamic and multicultural Chungking Mansions

Looking at it now, it is hard to believe that what lies behind the shambolic facade of **Chungking Mansions** was in the 1960s the height of luxury apartment living. By the 1980s it had degenerated into unkempt boarding houses, and all manner of vice went on there. The mid-1990s saw some renovation of its adjoining shopping arcade, and these days Chungking Mansions has cleaned up much of its act.

The tenement building is home to scores of Indian and South Asian restaurants – several of them have been operating for years and offer value and authenticity. **The Taj Mahal Club** (3/F, Block B; tel: 2722 5454), **Khyber Pass** (7/F, Block E; tel: 2721 2786) and **Delhi Club** (3/F, Block C; tel: 2368 1682) are all reliable for samosas, naan bread, rice, curry, tandoor dishes, dal, lassis and a Kingfisher beer or two.

Clothing and all manner of traded goods can be bought from ground-floor wholesalers. On the same level are African traders and cafés and dessert shops that cater to halal observers. There are a couple of very reasonably priced internet cafés and SIM-card providers, as well as money-changing operations.

Do not be put off by the cast of characters that hangs around its entrance – some will immediately produce restaurant cards, presuming visitors are there for a meal. It is completely safe to visit.

Chungking Mansions; 36–44 Nathan Road; www.chungkingmansions.com.hk; map C1/2

Leave urban Kowloon behind and hike up to Lion Rock Country Park

Lion Rock Country Park is one of a few local city escapes that whisk you quickly from street to sky. In no time at all you can leave the bustle of traffic and pedestrians behind and reach this rugged upland region that connects North Kowloon and Sha Tin in the New Territories.

From a distance Lion Rock, the 495-metre (1624ft) peak which gives the park its name, really does resemble a maned head in profile. It is edged by trails both on the east and west sides – comfortable walking shoes and water are all that you need.

The park is easily reached from either Wong Tai Sin or Kowloon Tong MTR stations. It is signposted from the former, and takes around 10 minutes or so on foot; or it's a five-minute taxi ride from Kowloon Tong.

Ascend above the residential apartment blocks and once you've reached the summit you are rewarded with stunning views across Kowloon and Victoria Harbour to Hong Kong Island. Soak up the sights, listen to the birdsong and look out for the few roaming macaques up here. In some small sections of the hillside above Wong Tai Sin, local walkers have attempted to tame nature, creating their own little landscaped areas.

The more serious climber can scale vertiginous Lion Rock itself on either its east or west face.
Lion Rock Country Park; www.afcd.gov. hk; map C8

NEW TERRITORIES

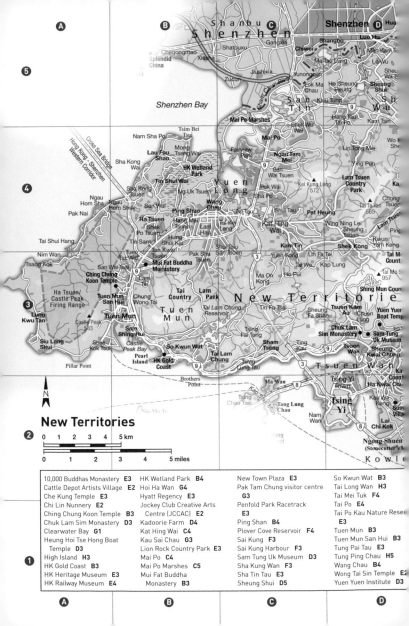

New Territories

Swing a golf club in the midst of stunning scenery at Kau Sai Chau

More courses

Good concierges should be able to swing you a favour on greens elsewhere, but two other clubs allow visitors and can be booked independently: also in the New Territories, **Clearwater Bay Golf & Country Club** (139 Tai Au Mun Road, Clearwater Bay; tel: 2335 3700; www.cwbgolf.org) and, over on Lantau Island, **Discovery Bay Golf Club** (tel: 2987 3750; www.dbgc.hk). Both clubs are very scenic, with restaurants and everything a golfer might need to hire. Visitor access is on weekdays, though only for three days a week at Discovery Bay.

While an old-school flavour of privilege permeates most members-only golf courses, the public course at **Kau Sai Chau** is a rare down-to-earth treat. More-over, it is beautifully landscaped, having been sculpted on part of the small, verdant island of the same name in the eastern New Territories.

Get the MTR to Choi Hung, then a taxi or no. 92 bus to Sai Kung's small harbour, where the course has its own clearly marked pier. The 20-minute boat ride there and back is a pleasant experi-ence in itself: as the small vessel pulls out to semi-open water, Sai Kung harbour appears quite picturesque, with its fishing boats and sampans framed against a mountainous backdrop.

Kau Sai Chau has two 18-hole courses, and clubs, shoes, trolleys and caddies are all available for hire. There is also a large driving range, floodlit after twilight. Do note that out-of-town visitors can play on weekdays only – this is Hong Kong's sole public course, and is much in demand at week-ends and on public holidays.

Kau Sai Chau Public Golf Course; Sai Kung; tel: 2791 3388; www.kscgolf.org.hk; daily 7am–8pm; map G3

Catch your own squid on a trawler at night

Sai Kung harbour is lined with open-fronted seafood restaurants, which are a destination in themselves for many an urban Hong Konger.

A mind-boggling array of live marine life from local and overseas waters fills bubbling display aquariums: razor clams, horseshoe crabs and giant garoupa are some of the most eye-catching. Feel free to ask what's what and how it's cooked; steaming with ginger, spring onion and soy is a signature Cantonese method, although pan-frying, deep-frying and enhancing with chilli are also popular.

Some restaurants, and tour operators across Hong Kong, offer short evening cruises where you can hook your own squid and cuttlefish, which are taken ashore at the end of the expedition to be cooked in seafront restaurant kitchens as part of a set meal. A trip offshore at night is a tranquil experience, with the reflected Sai Kung waterfront shimmering about a kilometre away. This is a seasonal activity, as squid is particularly plentiful from around May to July. Catching squid is pretty much guaranteed: they are slow-moving, and attracted to the surface by light rather than bait. A recommended trip is with **Tung Kee** restaurant (96–102 Man Nin Street; tel: 2792 7493).

Boarding a boat is a fun end to a day in this laid-back town or at the beaches that are within easy reach. From restaurant tables at night, squid trawlers and their spotlights are always visible, dotted along the horizon.

Sai Kung harbour; map F3

Escape the crowds and head to a beautiful and tranquil beach

While Hong Kong's Southside beaches get fairly busy at weekends and holidays, some of those in the New Territories are more off the beaten track. Given the modest effort required to reach **Clearwater Bay**, the rewards are great: its well-maintained beaches are surrounded by hills and are seriously striking. The bay is a little busier at weekends, when pleasure boats drop anchor offshore.

Catch bus no. 91 from Diamond Hill MTR station and spend some time lazing on one of two long soft-sand stretches: if you are with kids, there is plenty of space here for them to let off steam. Simply named **Clearwater Bay First Beach** and **Second Beach**, there are lifeguards, showers and barbecue areas. Food supplies are limited to a kiosk on Second Beach, which also serves cooked dishes. Your best bet is to stock up at the **Park N Shop** supermarket in Plaza Hollywood above the MTR station.

Set back in the hills overlooking the beaches is Tai Hang Tun Barbecue Area, where barbecue and picnic facilities are provided, and there are some magnificent vistas out over the open sea. A popular kite-flying area on breezy days, it is also the starting point for several hiking trails up the peaks of Clearwater Bay Country Park. An easy-going 1.5km (1-mile) walk cuts across dense woodlands, with 15 information boards on plant life, and the chance to see plenty of butterflies and dragonflies.

Clearwater Bay; map G1

Gear yourself up for a demanding hike along the MacLehose Trail

Traversing the New Territories for 100km (62 miles) from west to east, the **MacLehose Trail** takes in the most dramatic mountain and coastal views in Hong Kong. Scrub-covered hills, occasional jutting rocky escarpments and reservoirs punctuate the western sections from Tai Lam Country Park in Tuen Mun, with one ridge after another spanning out to the eastern mangroves and sandy bays of Sai Kung Country Park, which the trail loops around to the east.

Pick up a detailed map and take on a section. In the west, 6.3km (4-mile) Route Twisk snakes from Tsuen Wan (map D3) to Lead Mine Pass, via Hong Kong's tallest peak, Tai Mo Shan. Its summit is often shrouded in cloud or mist – so pick a clear day for views across Kowloon and the New Territories. The Tsuen Wan starting point is best reached by taxi from the MTR station to Tsuen Kam Au; for Lead Mine Pass, catch a cab from Tai Po MTR (Kowloon-Canton Railway) station.

In the east, Pak Tam Chung Visitor Centre (map G3) is the start of numerous walks. Further east into Sai Kung East Country Park, the trail hugs High Island Reservoir, from where paths lead to several of the territory's most unspoilt beaches – including Tai Long Wan (see page 120). To reach the starting point, get a bus or minibus to Sai Kung from Diamond Hill or Choi Hung MTR stations; then get bus no. 94 bound for Wong Shek Pier, and alight at Pak Tam Chung.

Hop on a speedboat that will deliver you to a top beach and snorkelling spot

Reaching **Tai Long Wan** is quite a mission. From Wong Shek Pier, embark on a thrilling 15-minute speedboat ride round to Chek Keng, then join the MacLehose Trail (see page 119) and hike for an hour over the ridge to Hong Kong's most stunning bay where you are rewarded for your efforts.

There are two long swathes of pale, powdery sand, and usually enough surf to make it worth lugging a surfboard over the hill (the name means Big Wave Bay). But it is never crowded, and the water at the shore's edge is pretty calm, thanks to the colourful coral that breaks the waves. The water also teems with vibrant fish, and you can rent snorkels to observe them. Surfboards are also for hire, as are pitched tents for those who feel like stopping over – or bring your own. Modest restaurants and shower facilities are available.

To get to Wong Shek Pier, catch the bus from Diamond Hill or Choi Hung MTR stations to Sai Kung, then bus no. 94; or on Sundays and holidays, bus no. 96R from Diamond Hill via Sai Kung.

For even more pristine waters, head to **Hoi Ha Wan**, home to a protected marine park; two-thirds of Hong Kong's 88 hard coral species are found here, as well as a WWF starfish conservation project. Again, shops offer snorkel gear for hire. Eco-tours are given; see www.afcd.gov.hk. Get there on the no. 7 minibus from Sai Kung.

Tai Long Wan; map H3
Hoi Ha Wan; map G4

Share an evening with Sai Kung's expats in its cosy restaurants and pubs

The eastern New Territories town of **Sai Kung** has a similarly laid-back feel to some of the territory's outlying islands, but without the need to worry about ferry timetables. This neck of the woods has long had a small, loyal non-native community, who tend to commute into town from one of the 20 or so low-rise villages dotted around it.

As well as a host of waterfront seafood restaurants, Sai Kung has a smattering of cosy continental, Italian and other internationally flavoured bistros and bars, where you can mingle with the town's expat community and enjoy a relaxed end to a day trip around this area.

Takka Fusion Japanese Cuisine (15 Sha Tsui Path; tel: 2792 2202) has friendly staff and – besides straight Japanese items – some experimental deep-fried and grilled dishes that nod towards the restaurant name.

For Mediterranean-influenced food – think pizza, burgers and salads – long-standing **Jaspa's Restaurant** (13 Sha Tsui Path; tel: 2792 6388; http://casteloconcepts.com/our-venues/jaspas-sai-kung) draws locals back again and again. So does the casual café next door, **Ali Oli Bakery** (11 Sha Tsui Path; tel: 2792 2655; www.alioli.com.hk).

Of Sai Kung's few pubs and bars, **Duke of York** (18–32 Fuk Man Road; tel: 2420 0034) is a local favourite. Serving full English breakfasts in the mornings, it's a decent lunch spot and afternoon rarity in Hong Kong: it has a pool table.

Sai Kung; map F3

One-thirtyone

For a treat in the area, quality French restaurant **one-thirtyone** (131 Tseng Tau Village Road; tel: 2791 2684; www.one-thirtyone.com) is set in a converted three-storey village house on the quiet bay of Three Fathoms Cove. Surrounded by well-kept gardens, it is a great setting for a gastronomic treat or a romantic meal. The seasonal menu changes daily: expect home-made bread, and the likes of mushroom soup, pan-fried foie gras, cheeses and a trio of desserts. Advance bookings must be made.

Unleash your inner trainspotter at the Hong Kong Railway Museum

Its railway days ceased in 1983, but the renovated ticketing office and signalling room have been kept as true to the building's earliest years as possible. Other rooms display models of the evolution of both local and overseas trains. Real vintage locomotives and carriages in pristine condition can be inspected and boarded in the grounds – kids love them.

There are a few museums scattered around the New Territories, and the **Hong Kong Railway Museum** is perhaps the most charismatic, evoking some sense of what **Tai Po** may have been like before its full-on development as a New Town in the 1980s.

The museum's structure, with ornate upturned Chinese eaves and grey roof tiles, was formerly Tai Po Market Station; though at first glance, with its protective rooftop figurines, it might be mistaken for a traditional southern Chinese temple. It would have stood facing arable and livestock farmland when built in 1913. These days, Tai Po Market MTR station is just around the corner.

Another excellent museum in the New Territories is the **Hong Kong Heritage Museum** in Sha Tin, which contains a highly interactive mix of exhibits on history, art and culture – with specific focus on Hong Kong and Southern China. Little ones will enjoy the Children's Discovery Gallery. Six thematic galleries host regularly changing vibrant exhibitions, showcasing different corners of the territory and its environs, and explaining local traditions. The museum is signposted from Che Kung Temple MTR station.

Hong Kong Railway Museum; 13 Shung Tak Street, Tai Po Market; tel: 2653 3455; Wed–Sun 10am–5pm; free; map E4
Hong Kong Heritage Museum; 1 Man Lam Road, Sha Tin; tel: 2180 8188; www.heritagemuseum.gov.hk; Mon, Wed–Fri 10am–6pm, Sat–Sun and public hols till 7pm; charge, Wed free; map E3

Take a leisurely bike-ride along Tai Mei Tuk's lakeside cycle paths

Tai Po and its environs are a great place to head for some pedalling. Get there on the MTR, rent a bike from shops around Tai Po Market and embark on a 10km (6-mile) trip skirting the bases of Pat Sing Leng Country Park's sizeable mountains, northeast to **Tai Mei Tuk**. Here you can explore **Plover Cove Country Park**, with some of Hong Kong's finest natural scenery. For a more leisurely ride, get bus no. 75K from Tai Po Market to Tai Mei Tuk and rent a bike there.

Beautiful Plover Cove Reservoir was completed in 1968. A dam was built into the sea, with the resulting lake drained of seawater and filled with freshwater from newly created hillside channels. Today, you can cycle or walk between this fresh body on one side and the sea on the other. Heading north with the reservoir on your right, a beautiful path takes you through woodland rapids to Bride's Pool and Mirror Pool, each with plunging waterfalls.

Also in the vicinity is **Tai Po Kau Nature Reserve**, worth considering for serious hikers – a thick forest on a steep hillside. Get there on minibus no. 28K from Tai Po Market, bound for Sha Tin.

Tai Po; map E4
Plover Cove Reservoir; map F4
Tai Po Kau Nature Reserve; map E3

Combine dinner at the acclaimed Sha Tin 18 restaurant with a trip to the races

A few restaurants in Hong Kong offer quality menus that represent the cuisines of more than one region of China, and **Sha Tin 18** is a splendid example.

Its top regional Chinese chefs man separate kitchen stations in an open dining room at the Hyatt Regency hotel in Sha Tin. Northern Chinese and Cantonese cuisine is meticulously prepared. There's always something dynamic to watch, whether handmade noodles being stretched and cut or large woks frying, steaming and boiling. The Peking duck is a highlight, carved tableside and served as three courses: with pancakes; then chopped and stir-fried; and finally as a light broth.

Come on a Sunday and combine it with a day at the horse races, held every weekend at **Penfold Park Racetrack** except in the sultry summer months. You must be over 18 years of age and hold a valid passport. For a splurge, buy a Tourist Badge at the members' main entrance, which lets you take box seats, roam the members' betting halls and trackside areas and dine and drink at members-only outlets. The public stands offer an earthier experience, and the world's longest high-definition Diamond Vision television screen makes sure you catch every detail.

There are more food outlets to choose from at **New Town Plaza** mall, from noodle houses and cafés to vegetarian cuisine and Japanese restaurants. This complex also has some of the best shops on offer in the New Territories and a cinema.

Sha Tin 18; Hyatt Regency Hong Kong, Sha Tin, 18 Chak Cheung Street; tel: 3723 1234; map E3

Penfold Park Racetrack, Sha Tin; tel: 1817; www.hkjc.com; Sun, sometimes Wed and Sat 11am–6pm, races start after midday; charge; map E3

New Town Plaza; Sha Tin Centre Street; tel: 2608 7868; www.newtownplaza.com.hk; map E3

Improve your lot with a spin on the wheel of fortune or marvel at more than 10,000 Buddhas

Few modern cities take their traditional beliefs as seriously as Hong Kong, and the New Territories provide some good opportunities for you to get a temple fix.

Che Kung Temple is dedicated to Taoist deity General Che Kung, who quashed a rebellion in South China during the Sung dynasty (960–1279), and accompanied the Emperor when he fled to Hong Kong. After his death, people began worshipping him for his courage. The temple grounds feature a huge, ancient drum and bell. But most noteworthy is a copper fan-bladed wheel of fortune, which is believed to bring good luck when turned three times. Fortune-tellers can be found near the entrance.

A visit here is particularly enjoyable during the first three days of the Lunar New Year festival (its date varies yearly from January to February), when the atmosphere is animated, with local residents praying for good fortune in the year ahead or giving thanks for help in the previous one.

One of the most impressive temples in Hong Kong is in the New Territories: the **10,000 Buddhas Monastery**. There are actually more than 10,000 miniature Buddha images here, but in Cantonese tradition this number implies an inconceivably large amount. A visit to the temple provides some built-in exercise: the 431-step climb to reach it. The entrance is guarded by a variety of fearsome protectors, and inside a striking selection of gold Buddhas lines the walls. Elsewhere in the grounds is a nine-storey pagoda.

Che Kung Temple; 7 Che Kung Miu Road, Tai Wai; tel: 2603 4049; www.ctc.org.hk; daily 7am–6pm; free; map E3
10,000 Buddhas Monastery; 220 Pai Tau Village, Sha Tin; tel: 2691 1067; daily 9am–5pm; free; map E3

Cross a small moat to one of Hong Kong's last fortress communities

The walled villages of the New Territories trace their roots to the 10th century, when the 'five clans' built these fortified settlements to protect themselves from marauding outsiders, and each other. Later villages were occupied by the *Hakka,* Chinese migrants who moved here in the 17th to 18th centuries and lived apart from the Cantonese. The way of life in the walled villages remains fairly traditional, so it is worth paying the small donation to enter. The price for taking a picture of a *Hakka* woman wearing a traditional fringed hat will vary.

The most popular for visitors is the **Kat Hing Wai** village – to get there, take the MTR to Kam Sheung Road Station. Some 400 people live there, and most of them still share the same sur-name, Tang. Built in the 1600s, the fortified village shelters behind walls 6 metres (20ft) thick, with guard-houses at each corner, arrow slits for fighting off attackers, and a moat. There is still just one entrance, guarded by a heavy wrought-iron gate.

Over in Tsuen Wan, the **Sam Tung Uk Museum** was lived in by the Chan clan until they vacated the site in the 1980s and the government reconstructed it as a museum. Inside are rows of traditional houses and four original dwellings erected in 1786. There is also an ancestral memorial hall.

Kat Hing Wai Village; map C4
Sam Tung Uk Museum; Kwu Uk Lane, Tsuen Wan; tel: 2411 2001; www.heritagemuseum.gov.hk; Mon, Wed–Sun 10am–6pm; free; map D3

Embark on a guided tour of Kadoorie Farm animal conservation centre

Located to the west of Tai Po, **Kadoorie Farm & Botanic Garden** is about as far from urban Hong Kong as it is possible to get. Set up by the immigrant Kadoorie family in the 1950s to help local farmers, it has since evolved into a conservation centre and a pioneer of organic farming in Hong Kong.

More than half of Hong Kong's plant species grow here, and on the farm, pigs, cows and fowl are all kept and bred. Conservation projects include the rehabilitation of reptiles and birds of prey, and research enclosures include waterfowl, deer and butterflies. Make your own way there via Tai Po Market MTR and the no. 64K bus, or join a tour through local travel agents. Organic fresh and dry produce is also sold here.

Northwest of Kadoorie, occupying some of the last of the territory's wetland, are two other ecological zones: **Mai Po Marshes** and **Hong Kong Wetland Park**. Mai Po's 380-hectare (940-acre) marshes are the temporary home to rare migratory birds; WWF Hong Kong runs tours, as do some local travel agents. The 61-hectare (150-acre) Wetland Park, in Tin Shui Wai, is a world-class conservation site where you might spot egrets, kingfishers and black-faced spoonbills. Get the MTR to Tin Shui Wai, then Light Rail 705 to Wetland Park Station.

Kadoorie Farm & Botanic Garden; Lam Kam Road, Tai Po; tel: 2483 7200; www.kfbg.org.hk; daily 9.30am–5pm, by appointment only; free; map D4
Mai Po Marshes; Lok Ma Chau; visit through WWF Hong Kong; tel: 2482 5237; www.wwf.org.hk; charge; map C5
Hong Kong Wetland Park; Tin Shui Wai; tel: 3152 2666; www.wetlandpark.gov.hk; charge; map B4

Seek calm at Tsuen Wan's temples and monasteries

Off Tsuen Wan's **Lo Wai Road**, which leads to some of Hong Kong's less touristy monastery complexes, lies a quiet surprise.

Visible down a short shrub-covered slope, the white prow of a ship points its way forward along a boulder-strewn stream. At its prow, where a captain might stand, is a colourful upright statue of Kwan Kung, a fierce deity favoured by police, armed forces and even triads. At the stern is a serene white statue of Guan Yin, Goddess of Mercy; around her, plumes of smoke curl upwards at a red altar.

This may sound like a conceptual artwork lying in the landlocked northwest New Territories hills, but it is actually a living temple and shrine. On closer inspection, the whole 'vessel' is made of whitewashed concrete, and can be boarded by steps from a path. It has no official name, but characters on its side read **Heung Hoi Tse Hong Boat Temple**.

Head uphill for 100 metres/yds or so and on the opposite side of the same road is the **Yuen Yuen Institute**, a string of ornate structures that house a slew of Buddhist and Taoist deities and protectors. Its fishpond- and pagoda-punctuated grounds are also home to

a Confucian temple. The arches of all three religions are erected at the entrance of the institute, which was built in the 1950s. The main building of the institute, called the Great Temple of the Three Religions, is modelled on the architecture of the Temple of Heaven in Beijing, and in this temple deities of the three belief systems are enshrined. The complex is usually tranquil on weekdays, but weekends and public holidays are more bustling.

On any day, it is possible to hear the low-toned daily prayers of resident monks, or the meander-

ing percussion-accompanied horn harmonies played live as paper offerings are burnt in memory of the deceased. A vegetarian meal can be had here between 9am and 5pm. Get there via Tsuen Wan MTR station and minibus no. 81 from Shiu Wo to Yuen Yuen Institute.

A 2km (1.2-mile) walk west to Chuk Lam Sim (or by minibus 85 if coming from Tsuen Wan MTR Station, Exit B1), on Fu Yung Shan hill lies the small Buddhist **Chuk Lam Sim Monastery**, meaning Bamboo Forest Monastery. Built over a period of five decades from 1932, the monastery has a gallery of ink paintings and calligraphy by celebrated South China artists. Fringed by foothills, the tiered landscaping is lush, and well-spaced white-washed monastic buildings are connected by raised footpaths. Buddha statues in the main temple hall are some of the largest on display in Hong Kong.

Heung Hoi Tse Hong Boat Temple; 33 Lo Wai Road, Sam Dip Tam; map D3
Yuen Yuen Institute; Lo Wai Road; tel: 2492 2220; www.yuenyuen.org.hk; daily 8.30am–5.30pm; map D3
Chuk Lam Sim Monastery; Fu Yung Shan Road; tel: 2416 6557; daily 7.30am–5.30pm; map D3

Gaze across the shimmering marina at Gold Coast

Next to Castle Peak Bay in the northwest New Territories is the Mediterranean-themed resort complex called **Hong Kong Gold Coast**. European-inspired architecture dots Golden Beach, Hong Kong's first man-made beach, which stretches for more than half a kilometre. From the beach, a promenade leads to Dolphin Square, where it is often possible to spot rare local pink dolphins offshore.

The resort offers a different flavour to the everyday city bustle. Take your pick from a dozen or so restaurants at **Gold Coast Piazza**. All are open-fronted or -sided and overlook the bay and marina; the atmosphere is pretty laid back. **Killiney Kopitiam** (Shop F3, G/F; tel: 2194 6208; www.killiney.com.

hk) brings Singapore favourites: soup and fried noodles, curries and desserts. **Kung Fu Deluxe Dim Sum Kitchen** (Shop F5–6, G/F; tel: 2613 2380) offers what its name suggests – well, perhaps not deluxe but certainly tasty – and also serves up a wide range of Cantonese and other Chinese regional favourites.

At the **Yacht and Country Club** (tel: 2404 3257; www.gcycc.com.hk), yachts or motorised pleasure boats can be chartered and fishing trips arranged. To soak up the atmosphere at leisure, consider a stay at the laid-back waterside resort **Hong Kong Gold Coast Hotel** (www.sino-hotels.com/hk/gold-coast).
Hong Kong Gold Coast; 1 Castle Peak Road, Castle Peak Bay; www.goldcoast.com.hk; map B3

Marvel at the unique geology of Tung Ping Chau

Though really an 'outer island', **Tung Ping Chau** is one of two in the far-flung northeast of Hong Kong that doesn't have a ferry connection from Central, as this would be much too long a journey. In fact, lying some distance east of Mirs Bay, it's usually off the main maps and is just 3km (1.8 miles) off the Guangdong coast. From its hilltops, you get a panoramic view of the mainland's Bao An area.

Once supporting a population of close to 3,000, today Ping Chau is almost unpopulated, most islanders having moved to urban areas or emigrated years ago. The 2km (1.2-mile) long, mostly flat island, officially part of Plover Cove Country Park, is made of what are known as 'thousand-layer rocks' (comprising layered siltstone and chert) in different shapes and colours. There are other natural attractions as well, including caves and waterfalls, plus old-fashioned stone houses with courtyards and winding passages.

Coral heads lie just off a pristine sandy beach; the waters are bluer here than anywhere in Hong Kong and snorkels can be rented. Tai Tong Village has small restaurants and shops, and offers snorkelling and diving trips and simple accommodation.

A 90-minute ferry connection run by **Tsui Wah Ferry Service** (tel: 2272 2000; more info at www.geo park.gov.hk) is available on weekends and public holidays. From Sha Tin MTR Station, get the minibus to Ma Liu Shui ferry pier (ferries leave Sat 9am and 3.30pm, Sun 9am; return ferry from Tung Ping Chau both days is at 5.15pm).

Tung Ping Chau; map H5

SOUTHSIDE

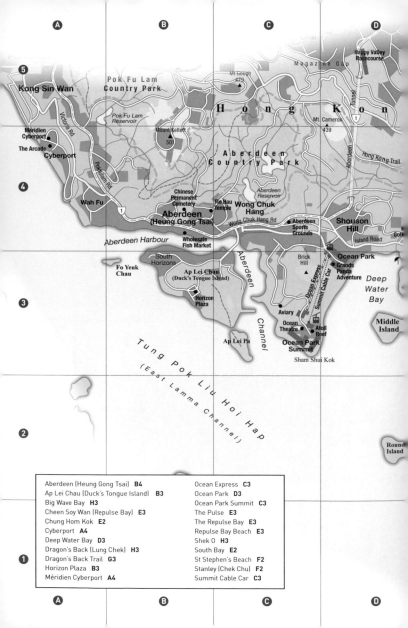

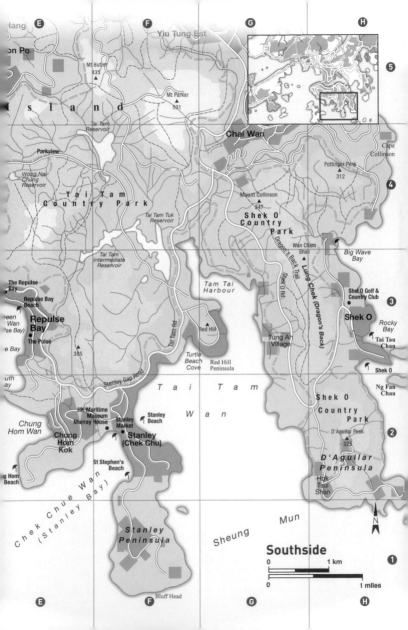

Whizz across the waves at Stanley, Deep Water Bay and Repulse Bay

In Southside you can skim the water's surface against a backdrop of golden sand, aquamarine sea and a sprinkling of rocky islands. Try water-skiing, wakeboarding or jet-skiing at **Stanley**, where there are two aqua sport centres, or a little further north at **Deep Water Bay** and adjacent **Repulse Bay**.

Stanley's two government-funded operations – **Main Beach**

Water Sports Centre (tel: 2813 9117) and **St Stephen's Beach Water Sports Centre** (tel: 2813 5407; www.lcsd.gov.hk/en/water-sport) – are hugely popular. The former faces Tai Tam Bay, whose relatively calm sea conditions in summer make it an ideal place for novices to acquire the basic skills; the latter's choppier waters year-round make it more of a challenge. You can wakeboard or water-ski at Deep Water and Repulse Bay with water-sport operators such as **SeaDynamics** (tel: 2604 4747; www.seadynamics.com). Serious water-skiers should contact the **Hong Kong Water Ski Association** (tel: 2504 8168; www.waterski. org.hk).

You'll notice gated low-rise and sparkling high-rise blocks set back off Deep Water and Repulse bays. These fetch staggering prices, with residents either from Hong Kong's most moneyed families or lucky expat contract workers.

Bus nos. 6, 6A and 260 from Exchange Square bus station in Central all serve Stanley, Deep Water and Repulse bays.

Stanley; map F2
Deep Water Bay; map D3
Repulse Bay; map E3

Be elegantly urbane by day or night at Repulse Bay

Across the road from the beach, on the site of the grand Repulse Bay Hotel, demolished in the 1980s, are the faux colonial walls of **The Repulse Bay** complex. The plush restaurants, spa and shops within hint at the elite splendour that once reigned here. Today, the most popular of Hong Kong Island's beaches has certainly lost all its airs and graces, but behind this replica facade you can still find a stylish air-conditioned getaway.

Two standout restaurants are **The Verandah** (tel: 2292 2822), where Continental fine dining takes place under tall ceilings and whirling fans; and **Spices** (tel: 2292 2821), which serves a pan-Asian menu both indoors and in its small garden. There is also a tastefully decked-out café and a quality supermarket, catering primarily to the residents of adjoining and nearby luxury flats.

The most recent addition to the area's restaurant and bar scene is **The Pulse**, home to a handful of contemporary beach-facing restaurants – a few with airy bar sections. Choose from the likes of **Hotshot** (tel: 2515 1661), a 'new American' casual Californian, and the sprawling **Limewood** (tel: 2866 8668), popular during the weekend for its international menu and cocktails.

Get a quality Southeast Asian experience right on the sand of Deep Water Bay at wooden-decked open-sided restaurant and lounge bar **Coco Thai**. Its chef hails from eastern Thailand and it's also a fine spot for sundowners.

The Repulse Bay; 109 Repulse Bay Road; www.therepulsebay.com; map E3
The Pulse; 28 Beach Road; tel: 2815 8888; thepulse.com.hk; map E3
Coco Thai; G/F, Beach Building, Deep Water Bay; tel: 2812 1826; www.toptables.com.hk; map D3

See the last of the floating fisher-folk families in Hong Kong

Bays and small harbours with jetties across Hong Kong were once home to thousands of boat dwellers. In Aberdeen, although there was a large-scale government programme to rehouse floating residents in flats in the same area, some families still remain in these moored wooden vessels.

From the promenade at Aberdeen Typhoon Shelter, you can see their houseboats at **Aberdeen Harbour**, moored next to each other in neat rows. For a closer look, you can charter a small wooden sampan – negotiate a reasonable sum (HK$60–80 for 20 minutes is about right) with the old ladies wearing wide-brimmed straw hats who beckon you on board. Weave between the remaining houseboats, which are often home to three generations of one family, a pet watchdog or two and even makeshift gardens of potted plants. Around 30 to 45 minutes will take you further around the harbour; if you have more time, you could request a one-way ride to nearby Sok Kwu Wan (40 minutes) or Yung Shue Wan on Lamma Island (one hour).

Back along the waterfront, some fisher-folk display and sell their dried seafood. There is also the small, dimly lit grey-brick **Tin Hau Temple**, which dates from the mid-19th century. As Tin Hau is the Goddess of the Sea and protector of those who sail on it, you can be sure that there will always be sticks and coils of incense burning here.

Leave the water's edge, cross the road and have lunch or dinner in the down-to-earth town, with its well-frequented fresh produce market and traditional medicine

Floating food and drink

With its interior decked out in as much lucky red and gold as possible, **Jumbo Kingdom** (Shum Wan Pier Drive, Wong Chuk Hang, Aberdeen; tel: 2553 9111; www.jumbokingdom. com) is best-known as Hong Kong's famous floating restaurant – but don't overlook its top-notch Cantonese fare.

From its own jetty in the middle of the Aberdeen Typhoon Shelter promenade, jump aboard the regular shuttle that putters the few minutes' journey to the restaurant and enjoy its signature seafood dishes that include sautéed fresh crab with chilli and garlic, and flambéed rice-wine-marinated prawns.

shops. **The Aberdeen Centre** (6–12 Nam Ning Street) is home to some decent eateries. For a Cantonese rice-based meal, try **Tai Hing** (Shop A, Phase 5; tel: 2552 9820), which specialises in roast pork and goose and has great, nutritious daily soups; or for dim sum and a full Cantonese repertoire, try **Hsin Kwong Restaurant** (2/F, Phase 3; tel: 2555 0388).

Get the MTR to Wong Chuk Hang station, or bus nos. 70 or 75 from Exchange Square bus station in Central go to Aberdeen.

Aberdeen; map B4

Pop into a converted warehouse block crammed with shops offering bargains galore

You wouldn't really guess **Ap Lei Chau** is a small islet, just offshore from Hong Kong Island, as it's linked by a flyover that joins it high above ground level. The main reason to detour over here (by MTR to South Horizons, bus no. 91 from Central or 92 from Causeway Bay) is to visit **Horizon Plaza**, a former warehouse packed to the gunnels with wholesale furniture stores, many specialising in Asian pieces both antique and reproduction, and a large number of designer fashion label discount stores. You can also bag fair-priced fabrics and home accessories, and even fine art, wine and foodstuffs.

Tequila Kola (1/F; tel: 2877 3295; www.tequilakola.com) was one of the pioneers. Its outdoor hardwood furniture, cushions, tablecloths and dining wear are modern with Asian accents. Chock-full of Western and Asian contemporary furniture, rugs, homeware and accessories and clothing, sprawling **Indigo Living** (6/F; tel: 2555 0540; www.indigo-living.com) also offers tableware and kids' home products.

For designer threads from a cross section of last season's popular fashion labels, head to Horizon's outpost of one of the city's favourite department stores: **Lane Crawford Warehouse** (25/F; tel: 2118 3403) stocks several international designer brands. There are many more labels on the building's upper floors.

Horizon Plaza; 2 Lee Wing Street, Ap Lei Chau; www.horizonplazahk.com; map B3

Dine within sight of a wide sandy beach at Shek O

After a pleasant day spent being a beach bum on a lovely stretch of fine sand, you can enjoy an equally laid-back evening at sleepy Shek O's Chinese, Asian and Western-style restaurants and pubs.

Many of Hong Kong's neigh-bourhood restaurants double as bars – especially when the venue is open to the elements at its front or sides. One such place is local favourite **Chinese & Thai** (no. 303; tel: 2809 4426), which serves as many large bottles of beer to its tables as it does food.

As you'd expect from the name, there's a split between its two cuisines – but there are more Thai listings. Fresh crunchy spring rolls and 'mixed fried rice' are popular, as are Thai chicken wrapped in *pandan* leaf, shrimp cakes, fish cakes and shrimp *tom yum* soup. This unpretentious menu hits the spot.

A drink at one of Hong Kong Island's few cult pubs, the **Black Sheep** (no. 330; tel: 2809 2021; www.blacksheepsheko.com), is recommended. The cosy, relaxed watering hole also has a reason-able European menu that is a notch above pub-grub standard – pizzas, grilled seafood and roasts are served.

To really feel 'on holiday', head onto the beach and choose from the barbecue pit restaurants: buy packs of fresh natural, marinated or seasoned meat, seafood and vegetables, charcoal and drinks and enjoy your own beachside party. **Lam Au BBQ Store** (tel: 2809 4793) has the best reputation for hygiene and flavoursome foods.

The fastest way to reach Shek O is to get the MTR to Shau Kei Wan station, then take bus no. 9 which terminates there. On Sundays and public holidays you can also take bus no. 309 from Central.

Shek O; map H3

Take a break at Stanley

When first arriving in the little Southside town of Stanley, the visitor is greeted with its ramshackle **market** (Stanley Village Road; daily 11am–6pm), with overruns of casual brands as well as winter and ski wear. The market is also a handy souvenir stop, with Chinese artwork, silk collectables, ornaments, carved stone seals and the like on offer. For some this is reason enough to visit; however, it's worth spending at least half a day here to take in the town's other diversions.

History buffs and those with an eye for aesthetics will enjoy the colonial arcades of **Murray House**, built as a British Army officers' mess in 1848. It originally stood in Central (on the site now occupied by the Bank of China), but in 1982 was dismantled stone by stone and put into storage. It was reassembled in Stanley in 2001. Today, it is home to a handful of international restaurants and bars. Styled on colonial Vietnam, **Ocean Rock Seafood & Tapas** (Shop 102, 1/F; tel: 2899 0858), with French doors that frame South China Sea views and tables that spill out onto a terrace, serves up a Mediterranean-leaning menu, as well as salads and grilled meat and seafood.

Right outside Murray House is **Blake's Pier**, also transported here from another location. Two, in fact: built in 1909 it was first a functioning pier on the Central harbourfront. Removed in the 1960s, it became a feature in a park in Wing Tai Sin, Kowloon – until it was transplanted to Stanley in 2006.

A 10-minute walk along the coast from Murray House is the more accessible of two temples dedicated to gods of the sea. **Pak Tai Temple**, built to look out to sea, is named after a Taoist deity favoured by fisherfolk who constructed it in 1805.

Stanley's main promenade is lined with restaurants and bars that get lively on weekends and holidays. Long-time favourite **The Boathouse** (86–88 Stanley Main Street; tel: 2813 4467) serves a reliable please-all Western menu and drinks list.

A relaxed day in Stanley can also include a sandy stroll and a swim at St Stephen's Beach (see page 136).

Stanley; map F2

142

Drop in on Southside's quieter, less-visited beaches

If the weather's good and the water's clear, Hong Kong's beaches are superb places to hang out. Not far from Hong Kong Island's favourite sandy stretches at Deep Water Bay and Repulse Bay (see page 136), **South Bay** and **Chung Hom Kok** are noticeably quieter and offer a more chilled-out beach experience. Both are sandy, and have lifeguards, changing rooms, showers, food kiosks and barbecue areas. Like all government-maintained beaches, they have roped-off swimming areas that are under watch by lifeguards as well as a netted boundary that keeps out sharks and a certain amount of flotsam too. There are offshore rafts to swim out to.

Set back from the main road with its traffic noise and dangers, both South Bay and Chung Hom Kok are popular with families – the latter particularly so, as it also has a decent beach playground and ex-cellent views towards Stanley Bay (this is the place to be at sunset). Chung Hom Kok is also popular with Hong Kong's gay community. There is a small ruined fortress just to the south.

On Saturday evenings and Sunday afternoons and evenings, South Bay takes on a party vibe, with some folk bringing their own drinks and tunes.

Buses do not run directly to either beach, so get a taxi or come via nearby Repulse Bay. Note that lifeguard services are suspended from November until March.

South Bay Beach; South Bay Road, Repulse Bay; map E2
Chung Hom Kok Beach; Chung Hom Kok Road; map E2

Take a hike along the Dragon's Back, culminating in a well-earned seaside meal or drink

Spend a rewarding couple of hours undertaking one of Hong Kong's most manageable hikes, which takes you across ridges with spectacular South China views. Part of the snaking Hong Kong Trail, this walk goes from urban Chai Wan to Big Wave Bay, a few minutes from Shek O and its handful of restaurants.

Catch the MTR to the eastern end of the Island Line, **Chai Wan**. Take exit A and head for signposted Cape Collinson Cemetery; take the steps that lead right up through the cemetery, which is on a hill. At the top of the hill, trail directions are signposted – head for Shek O. The walk ascends quickly, leaving the hum of the Hong Kong streets behind. Once you're up on the first grassy ridge,

several more undulate ahead, giving the Dragon's Back its name.

The walk along the dirt path, through scrub-covered terrain, is fairly gentle. As you reach sight of Shek O village and bay and descend the path, you are likely to encounter remote-control aeroplane and kite fliers, as well as the occasional paraglider.

The walk ends at **Big Wave Bay**, where a kiosk sells drinks and snacks and you can watch one of Hong Kong's few surf beaches in action. A 10-minute walk along the road leading away from the beach are Shek O's restaurants and bars and buses back to Shau Kei Wan or Central (see page 141).

Dragon's Back; map G3

Come face to face with a rare red panda at Ocean Park

One of Southeast Asia's largest aquariums and theme parks and one of Hong Kong's oldest and best family attractions, **Ocean Park** has lost none of its appeal, due partly to its remarkable ability to reinvent itself. Since Hong Kong Disneyland (see page 154) arrived in 2005, Ocean Park has stepped up its game with great results.

Its four adorable red pandas look very much like foxes at first glance, with their ginger fur with white markings, right down to the pointed snout and ears and black whiskers; but their bushy tails are white with brown stripes. Check out the park's pair of giant pandas, too. In the same enclosure there is also a giant Chinese salamander – a bizarre, prehistoric-looking amphibious creature.

As well as some enormous, walk-around aquariums filled with stingrays, sharks, swordfish and turtles, you can catch shows starring trained sea lions and dolphins. All the wildlife and marine life in this park is humanely kept – with information boards constantly highlighting the fragility of the animals' natural environment.

Ocean Park also doubles as an amusement park, with two areas linked by your choice of either a scenic cable-car ride or the Ocean Express train, which simulates an underwater journey with porthole windows and LED display screens in the ceiling.

Other amusements include three roller-coasters, a water-rapid ride, The Flash – a G-force spinning circle that inverts those strapped in at 22 metres (72ft) – and a handful of others spanning the adrenaline-rush scale. The park adds VR elements to rides for limited periods. All are inclusive with admission, and age and height restrictions apply.

Catch the MTR to Ocean Park station or express bus no. 629 from Central Star Ferry, Pier 7 bus stop.
Ocean Park; Ocean Park Road, Aberdeen; tel: 3923 2323; www.oceanpark.com.hk; daily 10am–6pm; charge; map D3

LANTAU AND OUTER ISLANDS

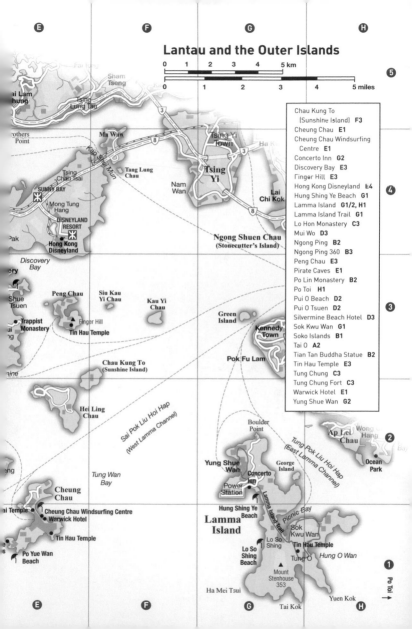

Lantau and the Outer Islands

0 1 2 3 4 5 km
0 1 2 3 4 5 miles

Chau Kung To
  (Sunshine Island) **F3**
Cheung Chau **E1**
Cheung Chau Windsurfing
  Centre **E1**
Concerto Inn **G2**
Discovery Bay **E3**
Finger Hill **E3**
Hong Kong Disneyland **E4**
Hung Shing Ye Beach **G1**
Lamma Island **G1/2, H1**
Lamma Island Trail **G1**
Lo Hon Monastery **C3**
Mui Wo **D3**
Ngong Ping **B2**
Ngong Ping 360 **B3**
Peng Chau **E3**
Pirate Caves **E1**
Po Lin Monastery **B2**
Po Toi **H1**
Pui O Beach **D2**
Pui O Tsuen **D2**
Silvermine Beach Hotel **D3**
Sok Kwu Wan **G1**
Soko Islands **B1**
Tai O **A2**
Tian Tan Buddha Statue **B2**
Tin Hau Temple **E3**
Tung Chung **C3**
Tung Chung Fort **C3**
Warwick Hotel **E1**
Yung Shue Wan **G2**

Be humbled by the world's tallest seated bronze Buddha at Po Lin

At the end of a network of hairpin bends, high above most of lesser-visited Lantau Island, is the red, orange and gold **Po Lin Monastery**, presided over by the world's largest outdoor seated bronze Buddha, at 34 metres (112ft) tall.

The Tian Tan deity, seated on a lotus leaf pad with a serene downward gaze, is reached by a climb up 268 steps from the monastery. Devout Buddhists from the world over visit all year – but in notably large numbers on Buddha's birthday in the summer (July or August, depending on the Lunar Calendar's tally with its Gregorian counterpart). The Buddha can often be glimpsed when arriving in or leaving Hong Kong by air during the daytime.

A walk in the monastery grounds is pleasant, especially on a weekday when it's less crowded; a vegetarian meal can be enjoyed in the refectory. To reach Po Lin, you can get the MTR to Tung Chung then bus no. 23 or the scenic Ngong Ping 360 cable car (see page 151); but if time allows, it's worth getting the ferry from Central Pier 6 to Mui Wo then minibus no. 2. The views from the switchbacks are impressive, and the journey builds up the anticipation of finally seeing the Buddha.

If you're after a less-visited Buddhist retreat, a three- to four-hour hike on the Lantau Trail westward from Po Lin leads to Ginger Mountain, home to quiet, brightly painted **Tsz Hing Monastery**, with its multi-tiered rooftops. Around halfway between Tsz Hing and Po Lin, paths down to Keung Shan Road connect with Mui Wo and Ngong Ping.

Po Lin Monastery; Ngong Ping, Lantau Island; tel: 2985 5248; monastery 9am–6pm, Buddha 10am–6pm, vegetarian meals all day; free; map B2

Take a memorable ride on the soaring Ngong Ping 360 cable car

The sightseeing **Ngong Ping 360** cable-car route stretches 5.7km (3.5 miles) up the side of a Lantau mountain from Tung Chung to the Ngong Ping Plateau, a five-minute walk from the giant Buddha above Po Lin Monastery (see page 150). This makes it the biggest cableway in Asia, taking 25 minutes to complete in one direction; its name refers to the panorama you're treated to on board – with magnificent views across Lantau and beyond.

To further upgrade the experience, you can ride in a **Crystal Cabin**; of the 109 suspended capsules, these 37 have transparent flooring to enhance the sensation of floating. They also carry fewer passengers (10 rather than the standard 17). Included with a Crystal Cabin 360 package, or bookable separately, is a round-trip cable-car journey and admission to three attractions at Ngong Ping Village: *Walking with Buddha* is an animation that tells the story of the life of Siddhartha Gautama, the man who became Buddha; Motion 360 is a 4-D screening of a choice of two short films – the one about Lantau has superb aerial footage (as well as special in-seat effects); and Stage 360 is a rotating live show in a mini-theatre.

There are a few restaurants up here too, as well as nature trails; it's easy to make a day of it.

Ngong Ping 360 cable car; Ngong Ping, Lantau Island; tel: 3666 0606; www.np360. com.hk; Mon–Fri 10am–6pm, Sat–Sun 9am–6.30pm; charge; map B3

Eat a delicious lunch with the nuns and monks of Lo Hon Monastery

For a sharp contrast to the bustle of Hong Kong's urban locales, turn off all mobile communications and head for a monastery. **Lo Hon Monastery** is easier to reach than others, and it can make for a particularly enjoyable lunchtime.

The monastery is perched on a hill with sweeping views across the relatively new high-rises of Tung Chung Town to a wide bay. Take a stroll through its small tiered vegetable, plant and religious sculpture gardens and prayer halls. The main prayer hall contains three shiny brass seated Buddhas and a conical tower studded with miniature bronze Buddhas, each of

which bears the name of a donor family; the tower is turned daily to bless these families.

By now you'll have worked up an appetite for a vegetarian lunch (noon–3pm). Lunch is served for parties of 10 or more on weekdays, with no number restrictions on weekends and holidays. Mock meats made of bean curd are used in some dishes. Soups vary daily, as does the vegetable selection – but everything is very tasty.

A 30-minute stroll west along Shek Mun Kap Road is tiny, ancient **Tung Chung Fort**. Wander its cannon-peppered walls and small museum, which describes how the fishing village and farmland used to look, and the marine police outpost that once kept watch for marauders.

Both sights are served by Tung Chung MTR station, then mini-bus no. 34 (get off at Shek Mun Kap for the monastery or Sheung Ling Pei village for the fort); or take the ferry from Central Pier 6 to Mui Wo, then either bus no. 3 or 13 to Lo Hon Pavilion or the fort.

Lo Hon Monastery; tel: 2988 1419; free; map C3
Tung Chung Fort; next to Sheung Ling Pei village; Wed–Mon 10am–5pm; free; map C3

Visit the fishing village of Tai O, known for shrimp paste and its buildings on stilts

Being out on a limb on the west coast of Lantau Island has helped preserve the old fishing village of **Tai O**. Divided by a narrow tidal inlet, this ramshackle but charming low-rise village dots both banks, with narrow footpaths the only means of travelling through it.

Though partially devastated by a series of fires over several decades, many of the village's famous wooden-stilted houses remain, sitting above the sandy inlet that is fringed by some of the territory's last remaining mangrove coastline.

A weekend visit witnesses Tai O at its liveliest, when the market does a brisk trade in dried seafood, freshly caught fish and locally grown fruit. Shrimp paste is a speciality: fermented with garlic, chilli and other flavourings, it is worth snapping up to pep up vegetable and stir-fry dishes. Down-to-earth seafood restaurants offer good value.

There are two small art galleries, and a dark, incense-filled temple in honour of Kwan Tai, Taoist God of War. To reach Tai O, take bus no. 1 from Mui Wo or bus no. 11 from Tung Chung. Buses also go from Ngong Ping Village and packages to both Ngong Ping and Tai O are available through Ngong Ping 360's website (see page 151).

Tai O; Lantau Island; map A2

Dolphin spotting

Fishermen offer short dolphin-watching trips off the coast here – and boat tours to Tai O from Central often get you up close to the Chinese white variety. Registered charity **Hong Kong Dolphinwatch** (tel: 2984 1414; www.hkdolphin watch.com) monitors the movements of this dwindling species and sensitively conducts sightings, while explaining the dolphins' habits and plight.

All aboard the Disney train to Hong Kong's 'Magic Kingdom'

Long-awaited **Hong Kong Disneyland** launched in 2005 with its own specially commissioned MTR train from Sunny Bay station, some unique-to-Hong-Kong rides and a setting against a panoramic mountainous backdrop. Families with young children (up to about 13) will find the most to amuse here – and you can pack more into it with designated admission times by visiting the FastPass machines at the entrance of most park experiences. Staying in a Disneyland hotel offers priority passes for a number of rides and shows.

For a real splurge with a group of up to six guests over three years old, tours with a personal guide whisk visitors past queues straight onto rides. Additional benefits include the choice of appearing on a parade float or on stage, or a privileged private meet-and-greet session with two characters, plus some souvenirs. Tours last three or six hours, leaving plenty of time to eat at the handful of Western and Asian restaurants, watch live and 3-D film shows, jump on an 'Amazon River Cruise' peppered with lifelike robot animals or try yet more rides. Look out for seasonal special activities – park Easter-egg hunts for example, or photoshoots that include costume and make-up makeovers.

Split into seven zones, the compact park has more than enough to occupy a full day's visit. Toy Story Land is a winner with younger kids and the recent addition of Marvel superhero and *Star Wars* experiences and rides have brought further appeal for the older crowd. There are three hotels at the theme park for the very keen.

Hong Kong Disneyland; Lantau Island; tel: 1 830 830; www.hongkongdisneyland. com; Mon–Fri 10.30am–8pm, Sat–Sun 10am–9pm; charge; map E4

Take it easy at the bars and beaches of Mui Wo

One of the first things you notice when pulling into Lantau's **Mui Wo** (or Silvermine Bay) on the ferry is the open-fronted **China Bear** pub (3 Ngan Wan Road; tel: 2984 9720), from which tables spill out to the water's edge just left of the ferry terminal.

On any given evening or weekend lunchtime, expat and local regular patrons are usually up for a relaxed chat and are a good source of island information. If you want to catch a live Premier League football game or other major sporting event, a TV will probably be screening it here. The pub-grub menu includes good thin-crust house pizza and South-east Asian dishes.

The village also has a mix of Chinese and Western restaurants. Popular Turkish joint **Bahce** (Unit 19, Mui Wo Centre; tel: 2984 0222) serves satisfying meze and hot dishes like stuffed vine leaves, lamb kofte and fish kebabs. It also has a lively bar.

Away from Mui Wo stretches long sandy Silvermine Beach. It is a short bus ride to Tai O (see page 153), Po Lin Monastery (see page 150) or the unspoilt beaches of Cheung Sha and Pui O.

Get here on the ferry from Central Pier 6; check the ferry timetable at www.nwff.com.hk.

Mui Wo; Lantau Island; map D3

Windsurf or kite-board off a small island that takes water sports very seriously

Hong Kong territorial waters are sprinkled with more than 230 islands. Here's a chance to launch off one of the larger ones, **Cheung Chau** – on a windsurf board. Rent a board and throw up your sail if you are already proficient, or take a lesson if you're not, at the **Cheung Chau Windsurfing Centre**.

To get there, board the ferry at Pier 5 in Central (check the timetable at www.nwff.com.

hk), then once you've alighted at the Cheung Chau terminal take the shortish path that crosses the narrow populated isle – it's around a 10-minute walk. When you get to the island's main beach, **Tung Wan**, walk to the headland on the right – the centre is just behind it.

Classes plus board and wetsuit hire can be arranged for blocks of a few hours or the whole day. Kite-boarding is also available for novice level upwards; this involves the dual skill of flying a glider-like kite on a cord that pulls the rider through water on a compact board. Both sports can be taught in group or individual lessons, and around a week's notice is preferred. The centre has a restaurant, open to anyone, serving a Mediterranean menu.

Cheung Chau has taken windsurfing a little more seriously than elsewhere in the territory since one of its own top enthusiasts, Lee Lai-shan, picked up the gold medal at the 1996 Olympic Games in Atlanta, USA. This was Hong Kong's first ever Olympic medal.

Cheung Chau Windsurfing Centre; 1 Hak Pai Road, Cheung Chau; tel: 2981 8316; www.ccwindc.com.hk; charge; map E1

Soak up the waterfront atmosphere or catch a festival on Cheung Chau

Dumbbell-shaped **Cheung Chau**, just south of Lantau, offers some good walks, fine beaches and a handful of temples dedicated to Tin Hau, Goddess of the Sea.

Cheung Chau village has a lively waterfront atmosphere. The waterfront promenade, the *praya*, is one of Hong Kong's most pleasant alfresco dining spots, especially after sunset. Head off in any direction from the ferry terminal and you will find both modern and traditional shops and restaurants. The village, around the ferry dock, is a tangle of interesting alleyways. Bicycles can be rented for around HK$20–30 per hour, on which you could zip round most of the island's paths within a few hours.

The island is also known for throwing some of Hong Kong's most exuberant and colourful festivals; the annual showpiece, usually in April or May, is the exciting **Cheung Chau Bun Festival**, during which the island's residents try to dispel what are known as 'hungry ghosts'. This involves a spectacular parade and a race up a tall tower covered in steamed buns.

Cheung Chau Island; map E1

Pirate loot

Ruthless 19th-century plunderer Cheung Po Tsai and his crew are said to have stashed their loot in the pirate caves of Cheung Chau Island. The treasure is thought to remain undiscovered to this day, so a trip here could net you a tidy windfall. To reach the narrow vertiginous caves, turn right when you disembark the ferry and follow the coastal path for about 20 minutes. The slightly inclined route is signposted and offers fine views over the craggy shoreline. Signboards announce your arrival at the caverns.

Escape the city and head to a charming, tiny island

Pack your book and and hop aboard a ferry from Central Pier 6 (ferry schedule: www.hkkf.com.hk) to the very low-rise and low-population **Peng Chau Island**. With its gentle walking paths and handful of restaurants and pubs, this is an archetypal island retreat – just half an hour from Central.

This tiny island of a little less than one square kilometre lies within sight of the northeastern shore of Lantau – from some parts of the isle you can make out Lantau's Discovery Bay. Like Lamma and Cheung Chau Islands, it has no roads; instead, footpaths crisscross it. You could easily see all the sights within a couple of hours, but it's worth staying longer and unravelling its low-key charms.

Like most of Hong Kong's inhabited islands, fishing was once

Peng Chau's mainstay, and is still evident in the moored boats with nets on deck. The island was once a centre for small-scale industrial production, and as such, parts of the main village are not particularly attractive – but most of its small alleyways and scattered heritage buildings do have appeal.

The Tin Hau Temple on Wing On Street, very near the ferry pier, is more than 200 years old. Tin Hau, Goddess of the Sea, takes pride of place at a golden altar near a huge whale bone – an ancient offering from local fishermen.

A little southeast of the village is **Finger Hill**; the short, steep climb rewards you with panoramic views of Tsing Ma Bridge, Lantau and Lamma Islands and southwest Hong Kong Island.

Peng Chau Island; map E3

Strap on your walking shoes for a hike from Mui Wo to Pui O

An exhilarating three-hour walk on Lantau Island takes you from **Mui Wo** (see page 155) over mountains to the fine long beach at **Pui O**. Both ends of this hike have restaurants, so you can start with a meal, end with one, or do a double dine.

This 15km (9-mile) or so segment of the 70km (43-mile) Lantau Trail rises immediately from a path at the town end of Mui Wo's Silvermine Bay, winds through woodland, then up to breezy shrub-covered hillside where ocean and mountain views abound. This section of the trail never rises much higher than around 450 metres (1476ft). Make sure you bring water; there are no shops for a few hours. Looking towards the centre of the island at certain points on the undulating path, you can see its two tallest mountains, Lantau and Sunset

Peaks, rising to 934 (3064ft) and 869 metres (2851ft). They also lie on the Lantau Trail and can be climbed.

The end of this walk dips down towards the small estuary and long wide sandy stretch of Pui O. Of the few small shops and cafés, a local no-nonsense Cantonese favourite is **Mau Kee Restaurant** (tel: 2984 1175), good for hearty noodle dishes. Most enjoyable, perhaps, for a full-on beach experience is **Mavericks** (tel: 2984 1328), just off the sand and serving a casual Western menu – service is very chilled, so don't be in a hurry. It's the perfect spot for an ocean-view sundowner.

From Pui O, you could get bus no. 1 (or 7P at weekends) back to Mui Wo; or bus nos. 3 or 3M, or a taxi, to Tung Chung.

Mui Wo; map D3
Pui O; map D2

Traverse two hills, from Yung Shue Wan to Sok Kwu Wan, on Lamma Island

The hills, beaches and international cafés of Lamma Island, lying around half an hour away from Central, make for a perfect contrast to urban Hong Kong. **Yung Shue Wan** and **Sok Kwu Wan**, its two small ferry terminal ports, are connected by a trail that dips up and down two manageable hills. The signposted walk takes around one hour.

You can get the ferry from Central Pier 4 to either Yung Shue Wan or Sok Kwu Wan (see www.hkkf. com.hk for timetables). Yung Shue Wan, home to a multicultural mix of residents, is the most populated of Lamma Island's villages and has something of a Mediterranean feel, with flats and houses climbing up a small hill and open-sided restaurants hugging the curve of the harbour wall. There is a Tin Hau (Goddess of the Sea) temple, where offerings of incense, fruit and food are made. If you're in Yung Shue Wan before 10am, Main Street buzzes with fishermen selling their catches and makeshift stalls touting fruit and vegetables, dried herbs and seafood, and no-nonsense clothing and homeware.

Take a stroll literally through the seafood restaurants along Main Street – the sole access path cuts through eateries whose kitchens and indoor tables are on one side, and alfresco seafront tables on the other. Like all of these, **Sampan Seafood Restaurant** (no. 16; tel: 2982 2388), the second one you reach from the ferry pier, has bubbling aquariums, packed with fish, molluscs and crustaceans. The steamed fish, stir-fried crab, salt and pepper deep-fried bean curd and dim sum are all good, as are the prices. Of the international selection, **Hideout** (no. 77; tel: 2982 4321) often feels like a private dining room. Its intimate terrace and interior have a clean contemporary look and the small menu – great burgers and pasta – really hits the spot. With

a bohemian air, **Bookworm Café** (no. 79; tel: 2982 4838) serves up Western-style vegetarian dishes; enjoy a hearty veggie lasagne, meze plate or organic salad here. Cakes at tea time are usually top notch with an organic tea or coffee.

Some 25 minutes' walk from Yung Shue Wan's ferry pier, past some three-storey buildings and neat vegetable plots, **Hung Shing Yeh Beach** is a good stopping point. There is a terrace restaurant here at the small hotel **Concerto Inn** (28 Hung Shing Yeh Beach; tel: 2982 1668; www.concertoinn.com.hk).

From here, follow the marked trail for a further half-hour, passing dirt paths that lead to beautiful beaches such as signposted **Lo So Shing** and to Lamma's tallest peak, Mount Stenhouse (353 metres/1158ft).

On the way into less-populated Sok Kwu Wan, you pass a Tin Hau temple. Further on, quality seafood restaurants line the waterfront all the way to the ferry pier. **Rainbow** (23–25 First Street; tel: 2982 8100; lammarainbow.com) serves up garlic prawns and lobster in 10 kinds of butter; and **Wai Kee Seafood Restaurant** (3–4 First Street; tel: 2982 8135) is a reliable favourite. Take your pick, watch the boats come in, and, when sated, jump on one back to Central.

Lamma Island; map G1/2, H1

Hire a junk to visit off-the-beaten-track Po Toi Island – or view it from the comfort of your boat

Po Toi, one of the smallest inhabited islands in Hong Kong, lies in its southernmost territorial waters. Though served by a sporadic public ferry at weekends, it makes a decent destination for chartering a junk – a small wooden pleasure boat – or a white fibreglass vessel.

These kinds of pleasure boats can come with catering, or you may opt instead to hop off and eat ashore. Prices for a day's hire start at around HK$4,800; some operators will offer half-day rates. Most boats have a few snorkel and mask sets, large rubber rings for quick dips, and a freshwater shower; often there is also a small motorised dinghy for shuttling to shore.

Junk and pleasure boat hirers with good reputations include **Sea**

Lagoon (Room 1104, Crawford House, 70 Queen's Road Central, Central; tel: 2165 4196; www.sea lagoon.com), which has a range of vessels; **Lazy Days** (tel: 3488 1534; www.lazydays.com.hk); and **Duk Ling** (Unit 914, 9/F, Tower A, New Mandarin Plaza, 14 Science Museum Road, Tsim Sha Tsui East; tel: 3759 7079; www.dukling.com.hk). The first two rent boats of different sizes and can arrange catering and drinks packages; the latter hires out one characterful vessel, the red-sailed (but still motorised) *Duk Ling*, with painstakingly renovated 50-year-old decks in the same design as junks built in the mid-19th century.

You may prefer to simply view Po Toi from the comfort of your hired vessel, but if you do go ashore, the island is laced with a few dramatic coastal paths; the best leads to a stark granite headland where cliffs drop away into the surging South China Sea below. A gentler hike heads over rough internal hill trails where kites, white-bellied sea eagles and gulls fly overhead.

In the small village are a few seafood restaurants offering tasty meals with an excellent sea view; nearby there's a **Tin Hau Temple** that is more than 150 years old.
Po Toi Island; map H1

Spend Saturday night bar-hopping the friendly pubs in Lamma Island's Yung Shue Wan

Saturday night on some of Hong Kong's outlying islands can be pretty quiet. Luckily, Lamma Island's busiest village Yung Shue Wan has some great pubs – and they're all within staggering distance along Main Street.

From the ferry pier, three pubs punctuate the path. Patrons from **The Island Bar** (no. 6; tel: 2982 1376), right next to the pier, regularly clog the path on weekend evenings, when they stand outside and spill into a small public garden opposite. This most lively of Lamma pubs regularly has bands playing its tiny stage. You can see ferries coming in from here and be on one within a few minutes.

Transplanted from Wan Chai a few years ago, **Blue Goose Tavern** (no. 18; tel: 2982 1688) has a Brit pub feel inside, with a pool table upstairs and waterside tables gracing a back terrace. **Jing Jing Bar** (no. 51; tel: 3480 0012) is a cosy one, with a tiny terrace outside. At all venues, English Premiership football, international

football and rugby games are often screened live; at these times the atmosphere is pretty animated.

Two small restaurants become relaxed watering holes by around 10pm. **The Waterfront** (no. 58; tel: 2982 1168), just off the main drag, has a canopied terrace on which you can enjoy tasty pastas, cottage pie and South Asian dishes. Regulars perch at the entrance bar, where there is a selection of draught pumps. **Lamma Grill** (no. 36; tel: 2982 1447; www.lammagrill.com) is a take on an American grillroom, with some Asian touches in its salads. Its slow-cooked pork ribs are particularly good. Sit waterside or indoors – where a band occasionally plays.

And if it's Indian food you're after, **Bombay Bar & Restaurant** (no. 6 Back Street; tel: 2982 0095; http://en-gb.facebook.com/bombay barrestaurant) serves quality tandooris and curry dishes.

Yung Shue Wan; map G2

ESSENTIALS

A

ADDRESSES

The ground floor is G/F, the one above 1/F (first floor) and so on, but address may be written '205' (for second floor, apartment 5).

B

BUSINESS CARDS

In business and similar situations in Hong Kong, you will be expected to present a business card. Present cards with both hands, and accept them the same way.

C

CHILDREN

Most five-star hotels offer babysitting services.

CLIMATE

Subtropical Hong Kong has four seasons:
Winter: late December to February; the weather varies from mild to cool, with some fog and rain – increasingly, there can be warmer days; 13°C (55°F) to 25°C (77°F), occasionally dipping below 10°C (50°F).
Spring: March to mid-May; damp, overcast and pleasant sunny days; 20°C (68°F) in March to 30°C (86°F) in May. Humidity is usually high.
Summer: Hazy, humid heat, punctuated by dramatic rainstorms, alternates

with clearer days; usually above 30°C (86°F), and 80–90 percent humidity day and night. July until September are peak typhoon months.
Autumn: A pleasant time to visit Hong Kong, with cooler, drier air. From late September, temperatures drop from 29°C (84°F) to around 20°C (68°F) in December.

CLOTHING

During the hottest months wear the lightest clothes possible and sandals. Bring a sweater or jacket for over-air-conditioned buildings. Temperatures vary sharply from one day to the next from November to April, so pack for warm and cool days, and dress in layers. Few buildings have heating, so it can seem colder inside than out.

CONSULATES AND VISA OFFICES

Australia: Consulate-General, 23–24/F Harbour Centre, 25 Harbour Road, Wan Chai; tel: 2827 8881; http://hong kong.china.embassy.gov.au.
Canada: 9th floor, Berkshire House, 25 Westlands Road, Quarry Bay; tel: 3719 4700; www.canadainternational. gc.ca.
New Zealand: 6501 Central Plaza, 18 Harbour Road, Wan Chai; tel: 2525 5044; www.nzembassy.com/hong-kong.
UK: Consulate-General, 1 Supreme Court Road, Admiralty; tel: 2901 3000; www.gov.uk/world/organisations/british-consulate-general-hong-kong.

USA: Consulate-General, 26 Garden Road, Central; tel: 2523 9011; http://hk.usconsulate.gov.

Mainland China

Office of the Commissioner of the Ministry of Foreign Affairs Visa Application Service Centre, 20th floor, AXA Centre, 151 Gloucester Road, Wan Chai; tel: 2992 1999; www.visaforchina.org. Two photos are required, and single entry visas cost from HK$250 (depending on nationality), and are processed in about three days. China visas can also be obtained through many Hong Kong travel agents, for about double the cost.

CRIME AND SAFETY

Hong Kong has a low level of crime. In the main shopping and entertainment areas men and women can walk alone pretty safely at any hour. Tourists may be more obvious targets for pickpockets in busy areas, but normal basic precautions usually suffice.

CUSTOMS

Visitors over 18 can import almost anything for their personal use (including an unlimited amount of cash and wine), but only 19 cigarettes (or 1 cigar/25g of tobacco) and one litre of spirits. For further details, see www.customs.gov.hk.

D

DISABLED TRAVELLERS

Apart from the airport, big hotels and some newer buildings, Hong Kong is not easy for travellers with disabilities to navigate. Useful access information to public buildings and attractions is on the Hong Kong Tourism Board's website (www.discoverhongkong.com) and at its information centres. A guide to transport facilities is found at www.td.gov.hk. Taxis are often the easiest way to get around.

E

ELECTRICITY

Hong Kong's electrical system runs at 200/220 volts and 50 cycles AC. Sockets take British-style three-pin plugs.

EMERGENCY NUMBERS

General emergencies: 999 (for police, fire service or ambulance)
Police enquiries: 2527 7177
Hospital Authority: 2300 6555

H

HEALTH

No vaccinations are required to enter Hong Kong, but doctors often recommend immunisations against flu and tetanus. Tap water exceeds WHO standards, but bottled water may be more palatable and is widely available. For current information on influenza and other health concerns, see www.who.int/csr/en.

Medical services

Hong Kong's government health care system requires visitors to pay HK$1,230 if they use the Accident & Emergency services at public hospitals. For information on all medical services, call the Hospital Authority helpline, tel: 2300 6555, or visit www.ha.org.hk.

Hospitals

Queen Elizabeth Hospital:
30 Gascoigne Road, Kowloon; tel: 2958 8888.
Queen Mary Hospital: 102 Pok Fu Lam Road, Hong Kong Island; tel: 2855 3838.
24-hour GP and outpatient service at private **Hong Kong Central Hospital**: 1B Lower Albert Road, Central; tel: 2522 3141.

Pharmacies

Pharmacies (identified by a red cross) are abundant, as are traditional Chinese herbalists. Pharmacies will only accept prescriptions issued by a doctor in Hong Kong.

HOLIDAYS

Hong Kong's public holidays combine Chinese, Christian and, more recently, Mainland days of note. Banks, offices, post offices and some shops are closed on the following days:
1 January: New Year's Day
Late January/February: Chinese (Lunar) New Year, a three-day holiday
March/April: Good Friday and Easter Monday
March/April: Ching Ming Festival
April/May: Buddha's Birthday
1 May: Labour Day
June: Tuen Ng (Dragon Boat) Festival
1 July: Hong Kong Special Administrative Region Establishment Day
September: Mid-Autumn Festival

1 October: China National Day
October: Chung Yeung Festival
25 December: Christmas Day
26 December: Boxing Day

HOURS

Offices generally open Monday to Friday 9am–5.30pm or 6pm, but some government offices open from 8.30am–4.30pm. Many business offices also work a half day (9am–1pm) on Saturdays. Banks are generally open Monday to Friday 9am–4.30pm, and Saturday 9am–12.30pm.

Mall shopping tends to go on between 10am and 9pm, but the major shopping districts of Causeway Bay and Tsim Sha Tsui stay open later, up to 11pm. Smaller local shops open earlier, and each market differs. Most shops open every day of the year, except during the Chinese New Year public holidays.

I

ID

Hong Kong residents are required to carry ID. Visitors should carry with them a form of photo identification, such as passport, or a photocopy of it.

INTERNET

Most hotels charge for in-room internet service. Free Wi-fi access is becoming more widespread all the time in hotels, and the government is building a citywide free GovWiFi network. You can also access the web for free with a Wi-fi code in many coffee shops and some restaurants and bars.

L

LANGUAGE

Hong Kong's official languages are Cantonese (predominantly) and English. Street names, public transport and utilities signage and government publications are bilingual, as are most notices and menus. Many organisations have trilingual announcements and information – Cantonese, English and Mandarin (*Putonghua*), China's 'national' language. Basic English is understood in most downtown areas.

LGBTQ TRAVELLERS

Hong Kong is still fairly conservative, and gay marriage is not yet an option in the territory, but there's a cosmopolitan LGBTQ scene, scattered around Central and Soho. For more on gay nightlife in Hong Kong visit www.travelgayasia.com.

The annual Hong Kong Pride Parade (hkpride.net) and Gay Games – to be held in Hong Kong in 2022 (www.gaygameshk2022.com) – also highlight the city's laissez-faire attitude.

M

MAPS

The Hong Kong Tourism Board (HKTB; www.discoverhongkong.com) Information Centres carry an extensive range of maps, and give away basic ones on arrival. The General Post Office, 2 Connaught Road, has a good choice of maps and guides in its ground-floor gift shop.

MEDIA

Newspapers and magazines

The South China Morning Post is the dominant English language newspaper. Tabloid-style *The Standard* is free, focuses on local business, but covers some world news. The local quarterly edition of *Time Out*, *is* useful to an extent for what's on, entertainment and culture-wise. Digital resources include the websites of Time Out, Sassy Hong Kong and Lifestyle Asia. Hotel bookshops, newspaper vendors at the Central Ferry Piers, Star Ferry TST and branches of Bookazine and Kelly & Walsh bookshops have a good selection of international newspapers and magazines.

Television

There are four terrestrial TV stations in Hong Kong; Viu TV (channel 96) and TVB Pearl are in English. Most programmes on the English-language stations are US shows or films; not much is produced locally in English, except news. Most hotels offer a mix of international cable and satellite channels.

Radio

Hong Kong's government radio broadcaster RTHK relays 24-hour news from the BBC World Service on its RTHK6 channel (675 kHz AM). There are regular English news bulletins on RTHK Radio 3 (567 AM/97.9 and 106.8 mHz FM), which airs current affairs, chat shows and pop music, and RTHK Radio 4 (97.6–98.9 mHz FM), which focuses on arts and culture. Other English-language programming comes and goes.

MONEY

The Hong Kong Dollar is pegged to the US dollar at around US$1 to HK$7.80. In mid-2018 HK dollar exchange rates were around HK$11 to £1 sterling or HK$9–10 to €1.

Banknotes vary slightly, being issued by HSBC, Standard Chartered Bank and the Bank of China in the following denominations: HK$1,000, HK$500, HK$100, HK$50, HK$20 and HK$10. Coins include HK$10, HK$5, HK$2, HK$1, 50 cents, 20 cents and 10 cents.

Hong Kong dollars are interchangeable with the Macau currency the Pataca (MOP), should you visit.

Changing money

The best places to change foreign currency are banks, which generally offer the best rates, although most will charge commission. Bank hours are Monday to Friday 9am–4.30pm, Saturday 9am–12.30pm. Money-changers and hotels are an alternative, but can have hefty charges. Street money-changers in Tsim Sha Tsui, Causeway Bay and Wan Chai stay open late.

Credit cards and ATMs

Major cards are accepted at most places. However, check the cash price in shops; it may be lower than for card purchases. In most markets, only cash is accepted. ATMs are plentiful.

P

POST

Hong Kong mail is fast and efficient. Stamps are normally bought at post offices, open Monday to Friday 9am–5pm, and Saturday mornings. Airmail stamps are also available at hotels, 7–11 and Circle-K convenience stores. For more information on mail services, tel: 2921 2222; www.hongkongpost.hk.

T

TELEPHONES

Coin-operated public telephone kiosks are a rarity, with most requiring prepaid cards (available at HKTB Information Centres, convenience stores and hotels) and some accepting credit cards. Many hotels charge for local calls from your hotel room.

The IDD code is 001, followed by the country code and number. Within Hong Kong, there are no area codes; numbers have eight digits.

Mobile (cell) phones

To avoid roaming charges, get a prepaid SIM card with a Hong Kong number and fixed number of minutes. Many phone providers, hotel business centres and convenience stores sell them. Call charges to Hong Kong mobile phone numbers are the same as those to landlines.

Telephone codes

Hong Kong from abroad **852**
Macau **853**
Mainland China **86**

Useful phone numbers

Hong Kong and international directory enquiries: 1081
International operator/collect calls: 10010
Hong Kong International Airport Information, in English (24 hours): 2181 0000

TIME

Hong Kong is eight hours ahead of GMT and 13 hours ahead of US Eastern Time. Unlike in Europe and the US, there is no daylight saving time, so from April to October the difference is reduced to seven hours ahead of London and 12 ahead of New York.

TIPPING

Most restaurants and hotels add a 10 percent service charge to bills automatically. It's common practice to round up restaurant bills to the nearest HK$10; larger gratuities are expected when no service charge has been added. Taxi fares, too, are often rounded up to the nearest dollar or two as a sufficient tip. Restroom attendants and doormen can be tipped in loose change, and HK$10–20 is enough for bellboys and room service.

TOURIST INFORMATION

HKTB has information booths at the airport, some ferry piers and land crossings, offering brochures and details of events around the territory, plus day and half-day tours run by HKTB. It also provides a multilingual visitor hotline, tel: 2508

1234 (daily 8am–6pm), and a comprehensive website: www.discover hongkong.com.

TRANSPORT

This city has an efficient, easy-to-use public transport system. Save money and time with a stored-value Octopus travel card. Over-65s and children aged under 12 travel half-fare on most transport, and under-3s travel free.

Arriving by air

Hong Kong International Airport at Chek Lap Kok on Lantau Island is about 34km (21 miles) from Central, Hong Kong Island. Immigration and baggage collection move swiftly. **Airport Information**: tel: 2181 8888; www.hongkongairport.com.

Transport to and from the airport

The Airport Express rail line, part of the MTR system, is the quickest and most convenient way into town, reaching Central station in 24 minutes, with stops at Tsing Yi and Kowloon. Trains run in both directions daily, from 5.50am–1am. Free shuttle buses run between Central and Kowloon Airport Express stations to many hotels, Hung Hom KCR train station and the China Ferry Terminal. Passengers can check in bags at Airport Express stations, up to two hours before departure.

There are also airport buses, and **taxis** are easy to find (costing around HK$370 to Hong Kong Island and less to Kowloon).

Arriving by sea

Cruise ships dock at the **Kai Tak Cruise Terminal** and **Ocean Terminal** in Tsim Sha Tsui, right next to the Star Ferry terminal.

Getting around: the MTR

The Mass Transit Railway (MTR) is a fast, clean, reasonably priced rail network that runs from around 5.50am–12.50am. Automatic machines dispense tickets or recharge Octopus cards at all stations. Everything is signposted in English and Chinese, and on-train stop announcements are multilingual. Stations have well-marked exits, identified by letters and numbers, so it's useful to have an idea of which you want; however, there are good local area maps at all stations. Information: tel: 2881 8888; www.mtr.com.hk.

Getting around: buses

Bus routes cover every part of the territory. Most run 6am–midnight, but some operate all night. Drivers rarely speak much English, but digital displays on most spell out stops in English and Chinese. Octopus cards or exact change must be paid on entry. You can pick up free maps of main bus routes at HKTB Information Centres.

Sixteen-seater minibuses are another option; but be cautious, as timetables are Chinese-only and stops are unannounced.

Getting around: trams

Trams skirt Hong Kong Island's north shore; the flat fare is paid as you get off (see page 38).

The **Peak Tram** is actually a funicular railway, up to the Peak Tower (see page 41).
Hong Kong Tramways: tel: 2548 7102; www.hktramways.com.
Peak Tram: tel: 2522 0922; www.thepeak.com.hk.

Getting around: Star ferries

No visit to Hong Kong is complete without a trip across Victoria Harbour on the green-and-white, open-sided Star Ferry; it runs daily 6.30am–11.30pm, taking about eight minutes between Central and Tsim Sha Tsui.
Star Ferry Information: tel: 2367 7065; www.starferry.com.hk.

Getting around: taxis

Taxis are easy to hail on the street, outside rush hours. They come in three colours: red on Hong Kong Island and Kowloon; green taxis run in the New Territories and blue ones on Lantau. The minimum fee for red taxis is HK$24, with extra charges for luggage placed in the car boot, booked taxis, and tunnel and bridge tolls. All fares are metered, and receipts given. By law passengers must wear seat belts. To call a taxi, tel: 2571 2929.

Ferries to the outlying islands

Ferries to Lamma, Lantau, Cheung Chau and Hong Kong's other islands leave from Piers 1–6 of the Central Ferry Piers, near the Star Ferry Piers in Central on Hong Kong Island.
Information: Ferries to Lamma and Peng Chau: tel: 2815 6063; www.hkkf.com.hk. To Cheung Chau, and

Lantau's Mui Wo: tel: 2131 8181; www.nwff.com.hk.

Ferries to Macau and Mainland China

Turbojet (tel: 2859 3333; www.turbo jet.com.hk) runs ferries 24 hours a day, 365 days a year to Macau from the Shun Tak Centre's Macau Ferry Terminal, west of the Central Ferry Piers; China Ferry Terminal in Tsim Sha Tsui, Kowloon; and Tuen Mun, New Territories. It also sails to ports in Mainland China from the latter two terminals. Cotai Jet (www.cotai waterjet.com) ferries run from the same Hong Kong Island and Kowloon locations in Hong Kong to the ferry terminal at Taipa.

Trains to the New Territories and Mainland China

The MTR network includes lines serving the New Territories. Trains are fast and frequent. Information: tel: 2881 8888; www.mtr.com.hk.

Several daily trains run from Hung Hom station in Kowloon to Guang-zhou via Shenzhen. There are also long-distance trains to Beijing or Shanghai every two days. If direct tickets to Guangzhou are sold out, take the East Rail line to the border at Lo Wu. Shenzhen station is a few minutes' walk.

V

VISAS

Most visitors only need a valid passport to enter Hong Kong. British citizens with full UK passports are given six months; nationals of other EU countries, Australia, Canada, New Zealand, the US and some other countries get three months. Hong Kong Immigration website: www.immd.gov.hk.

W

WEBSITES

Hong Kong Tourist Board: www.discoverhongkong.com.
Hong Kong SAR Leisure and Culture Department: www.lcsd.gov.hk.
Macau Tourist Office: www.macau tourism.gov.mo.

INDEX

Experience Hong Kong
Editor: Helen Fanthorpe
Author: Andrew Dembina
Update Production: Apa Digital
Head of DTP and Pre-Press: Rebeka Davies
Picture Editor: Tom Smyth
Cartography: original cartography James Macdonald, updated by Carte
Photography: 4Corners Images 1, 4/5, 6; Alamy 11, 29, 33, 42, 44/45, 47, 62, 64, 67, 94, 98, 103, 111, 118, 119, 128/129, 130, 137, 144, 158, 162; Alex Havret/Apa Publications 16B, 16T, 17, 32, 36, 40, 80, 84, 87, 92, 99, 125, 126, 127, 143, 155; Artelier de Joel Ruichon 39; Blue Bar 31; Bo Innovation 10; Cafe Gray Duluxe 37; Disneyland Hong Kong 154; Four Seasons 35; Getty Images 74, 77, 83, 102, 121, 138/139; Hin Mun Lee/Apa Publications 75; Honbo 81; Hong Kong Tourist Board 61, 68, 122, 123, 140, 157; Hyatt Hotels 78, 124; iSquare 93; iStock 21, 38, 41, 82, 106, 107, 110, 136, 146, 156, 159; James Tye/Apa Publications 65; Jockey Club Kau Sai Public Golf Course 116; Kayak and Hike.com 13T; Kenneth Lim 58; Leonardo 96, 101; Leung Cho Pan/Picfair 117; Mandarin Oriental 18, 34, 46, 86; Ming Tang-Evans/Apa Publications 8, 9B, 9T, 12, 13B, 14, 15, 19, 24, 30, 43, 48, 54, 55, 60, 62/63, 66, 70, 76, 79, 88, 97, 100, 108, 109, 112, 120, 132, 141, 142, 150, 152, 153; Shutterstock 56/57, 85, 131, 145, 151, 160/161, 163; Sky Shuttle 69; Starwood Hotels & Resorts 104; the Drop 53; Uma Nota 52
Cover: iStock

Distribution
UK, Ireland and Europe
Apa Publications (UK) Ltd
sales@insightguides.com
United States and Canada
Ingram Publisher Services
ips@ingramcontent.com
Australia and New Zealand
Woodslane
info@woodslane.com.au

Southeast Asia
Apa Publications (SN) Pte
singaporeoffice@insightguides.com
Worldwide
Apa Publications (UK) Ltd
sales@insightguides.com

Special Sales, Content Licensing and CoPublishing
Insight Guides can be purchased in bulk quantities at discounted prices. We can create special editions, personalised jackets and corporate imprints tailored to your needs.
sales@insightguides.com
www.insightguides.biz

First Edition 2018

All Rights Reserved
© 2018 Apa Digital (CH) AG and
Apa Publications (UK) Ltd

Printed in China by CTPS

Contact us
Every effort has been made to provide accurate information in this publication, but changes are inevitable. The publisher cannot be responsible for any resulting loss, inconvenience or injury. We would appreciate it if readers would call our attention to any errors or outdated information. We also welcome your suggestions; please contact us at:
hello@insightguides.com
www.insightguides.com

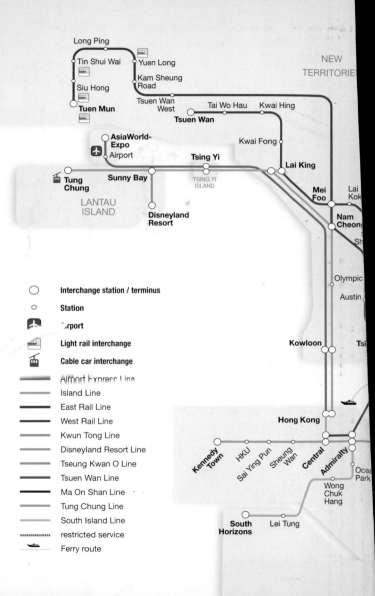

Long Ping
Tin Shui Wai
Yuen Long
Kam Sheung Road
Siu Hong
Tsuen Wan West
Tuen Mun
Tsuen Wan
Tai Wo Hau
Kwai Hing

AsiaWorld-Expo
Airport
Kwai Fong
Tsing Yi
Lai King

Tung Chung
Sunny Bay
TSING YI ISLAND
Mei Foo
Lai Kok

LANTAU ISLAND
Disneyland Resort
Nam Cheong
Sh

Olympic

Austin

○ Interchange station / terminus
○ Station
Airport
Light rail interchange
Cable car interchange
Airport Express Line
Island Line
East Rail Line
West Rail Line
Kwun Tong Line
Disneyland Resort Line
Tseung Kwan O Line
Tsuen Wan Line
Ma On Shan Line
Tung Chung Line
South Island Line
restricted service
Ferry route

Kowloon
Tsi

Hong Kong
Kennedy Town
HKU
Sai Ying Pun
Sheung Wan
Central
Admiralty
Ocea Park

Wong Chuk Hang

South Horizons
Lei Tung